"Fleming Rutledge tells of a friend in her neighborhood who stayed away from church because she 'would have to look up at that big cross they have behind the altar with that figure of Christ hanging on it. It would upset me terribly' (*Bread and Wine*). Philip Jamieson hits the nail precisely on the head of this scandal of the cross that provoked such shame and outrage in the first centuries of Christianity in Greco-Roman culture. Jamieson sketches a convincing, gripping picture of contemporary American culture, riddled with and crippled by what he describes as the Kingdom of Shame—a society that yet remains clueless to this dominion of misery that undergirds and attends humanity's alienation from God and fellow human beings. As it turns out, Rutledge could never persuade her friend to identify the shame she felt looking at the public execution of Jesus with her own failings, weaknesses, or flaws, or dare she add, her own shame! In Jamieson's beautifully woven tapestry of God's redemption of human shame and shamelessness, this pastoral theologian shows the church how to recapture the scandal of the cross by reclaiming the face of the crucified Christ—bearing and breaking under the weight of all of humanity's shame-filled behavior, yet never turning away from the sunken faces of their godforsakenness in his solidarity with them. God was in Christ being shamed to death for humanity's sake. To look up and gaze upon this face is to become transformed by the love that not even the rupture of godforsakenness within the relations of Father–Son–Holy Spirit could finally overcome. Jamieson's *The Face of Forgiveness* is a godsend to a church desperately in need of the forgiving grace of this saving face!"

David P. Moessner, A. A. Bradford Chair of Religion, Texas Christian University

"Phil Jamieson's *The Face of Forgiveness* offers a helpful theological distinction between guilt and shame. Jamieson effectively unveils some of the limitations of our therapeutic methods in dealing with the reality of our sin and brokenness and redirects us through a trinitarian perspective to a more wholistic model of healing. In particular, his description of atonement theories and exegesis of the cross is refreshing in giving substantive and spiritual impetus to the pastoral task of reconciliation. This book contains the necessary blend of prophetic and pastoral guidance to challenge and deepen our faith practice in the gospel work of redemptive healing."

Davis Chappell, senior pastor, Brentwood United Methodist Church

"Philip Jamieson has written a very important book. Here is pastoral theology built on the ministry of the triune God of grace as understood within the ecumenical sweep of classical theology. In particular, here is pastoral theology in close dialogue with the atonement developed in trinitarian and incarnational terms. Jamieson recasts the work of pastoral care as helping each other face Christ who is God's assurance of God's love for us. The issue all along—shame—has been fear of the loss of love. With this book Jamieson stakes out a bold claim for pastoral theology as theology, and as such, thankfully, can attest to the redemption of shame as we behold ourselves in the eyes of Christ."

Andrew Purves, Jean and Nancy Davis Professor Emeritus of Historical Theology, Pittsburgh Theological Seminary

"Jamieson joins others in noting that society is abandoning talk of sin. Rather than only pointing the finger outward he explores how Christian theology itself has contributed to this loss. He engagingly weaves together input from social science, theological reflection and pastoral application. Connecting the cross to shame is imperative in our context today. This book is a good place to start or a means of adding new insights to an atonement theology that addresses shame."

Mark D. Baker, Fresno Pacific Biblical Seminary

"Philip D. Jamieson's work *The Face of Forgiveness* is a wise and winsome account of a theme often neglected in pastoral care and theology. Jamieson contends that it is not simply sin and guilt that tears at human hearts and minds. Shame is just as destructive, for it pierces who we are. This book is theologically rich, pastorally insightful and carefully written. At the heart of the book, scholars and pastors will find a deep trinitarian account of how Christ's incarnation, crucifixion, resurrection and ascension heal human shame. Jamieson's profound and compelling work is pastoral theology at its best, drawn from a deep well of scholarship and wide-ranging pastoral practice."

Elmer M. Colyer, professor of systematic theology, Stanley Professor of Wesley Studies, The University of Dubuque Theological Seminary

"In this fine little book, Jamieson offers a Christ-centered reframing of forgiveness that shows how shame exceeds guilt as humanity's worst predicament before God and one another, and how the face of Christ provides the best therapeutic remedy. A good example of both pastoral theology and Christian psychology, the work strongly reflects a scripturally-driven agenda and the author's Christian theological tradition, both of which shape how contemporary psychology is skillfully interpreted and appropriated, while noting its worldview biases and limitations. Highly recommended."

Eric L. Johnson, Lawrence and Charlotte Hoover Professor of Pastoral Care, The Southern Baptist Theological Seminary

THE FACE OF
FORGIVENESS

A PASTORAL THEOLOGY OF

SHAME AND REDEMPTION

PHILIP D. JAMIESON

IVP Academic

An imprint of InterVarsity Press
Downers Grove, Illinois

InterVarsity Press
P.O. Box 1400, Downers Grove, IL 60515-1426
ivpress.com
email@ivpress.com

InterVarsity Press® is the book-publishing division of InterVarsity Christian Fellowship/USA®, a movement of students and faculty active on campus at hundreds of universities, colleges and schools of nursing in the United States of America, and a member movement of the International Fellowship of Evangelical Students. For information about local and regional activities, visit intervarsity.org.

Scripture quotations, unless otherwise noted, are from the New Revised Standard Version of the Bible, copyright 1989 by the Division of Christian Education of the National Council of the Churches of Christ in the USA. Used by permission. All rights reserved.

While any stories in this book are true, some names and identifying information may have been changed to protect the privacy of individuals.

The song on pp. 103-4 is "How Deep the Father's Love for Us" by Stuart Townend © 1995 Thankyou Music (PRS) (adm. worldwide at CapitolCMGPublishing.com excluding Europe which is adm. by Integritymusic.com). All rights reserved. Used by permission.

Cover design: David Fassett
Interior design: Beth McGill
Images: Face of Jesus: © CNAC/MNAM/Dist. RMN-Grand Palais / Art Resource, NY
Jesus' face (interior) © Bernardo Ramonfaur / Dreamstime

ISBN 978-0-8308-4099-1 (print)
ISBN 978-0-8308-9953-1 (digital)

Printed in the United States of America ∞

Library of Congress Cataloging-in-Publication Data

Names: Jamieson, Philip D., author.
Title: The face of forgiveness : a pastoral theology of shame and redemption
  / Philip D. Jamieson.
Description: Downers Grove, IL : InterVarsity Press, [2016] | Includes
  bibliographical references and index.
Identifiers: LCCN 2016010693 (print) | LCCN 2016011632 (ebook) | ISBN
  9780830840991 (pbk. : alk. paper) | ISBN 9780830899531 (digital) | ISBN
  9780830899531 (eBook)
Subjects: LCSH: Forgiveness of sin. | Forgiveness—Religious
  aspects—Christianity. | Shame—Religious aspects—Christianity.
Classification: LCC BT795 .J28 2016 (print) | LCC BT795 (ebook) | DDC
  234/.5—dc23
LC record available at http://lccn.loc.gov/2016010693

P	20	19	18	17	16	15	14	13	12	11	10	9	8	7	6	5	4	3	2	1
Y	33	32	31	30	29	28	27	26	25	24	23	22	21	20	19	18	17	16		

For Janet

CONTENTS

Acknowledgments

As I reflect back on over a quarter century of ordained ministry, I have reached one principal conclusion and a secondary, yet very important, related truth. My one great insight is that the dying face of Jesus Christ reveals all that we need to know and can know of the reality of God. The incarnate Son is the fullness of God's self-revelation. Jesus Christ is the content of what God would have us know about himself. I think T. F. Torrance probably said it best when reflecting on the theology of his own mentor, Karl Barth:

> However, of this we can be perfectly certain: the blood of Christ, the incarnate Son of God who is perfectly and inseparably one in being and act with God the Father, means that God will never act toward any one in mercy and judgment at any time or in any other way than he has already acted in the Lord Jesus. There is no God behind the back of Jesus Christ, and no God but he who has shown us his face in the face of Jesus Christ, for Jesus Christ and the Father are one.[1]

Jesus alone reveals both the fullness of God and the necessary human response to God's reality. And even more precisely, Jesus' face is the face of eternal love, a love that is steadfast and sure. Jesus' face reveals the love that does not depend on reciprocation. Jesus' face does not look away from us, even when we are at our worst, when we are both subjectively and objectively lost in our sin. His love abides when all else would fail.

The secondary truth is completely dependent on the first one. Without a realization of the first, we dare not contemplate the second one. Only a strong conviction of the reliability of the first allows us to dare to ponder the second. That secondary, fully dependent truth is this: how I live my life, how I respond to my neighbor and to God's gracious overtures, will either empower or weaken my ability *to perceive* that first and primary truth. Put more directly, I cannot change God's love for me—Jesus' loving face will not turn away. But I can most certainly lose my way and forget that the eyes that will not turn aside from me and you are eyes of love. We can live our lives in such a way that the God who calls to us sounds like an enemy rather than our Beloved. To sense his approach is to desire to flee. This, it seems to me, is the heart of the human predicament. This is central to what, in the Christian tradition, we call sin.

Our sin causes us to mistake the God revealed in Christ for our destroyer rather than our Savior. Because of our sin, we are all quite proficient at finding ways to avoid the living reality of that God. Perhaps no one is better at that evasion than ministers and theologians like myself. We fit all too well the category that C. S. Lewis described in this way:

> There comes a moment when the children who have been playing at burglars hush suddenly: was that a *real* footstep in the hall? There comes a moment when people who have been dabbling in religion ("Man's search for God"!)

suddenly draw back. Supposing we really found Him? We never meant it to come to *that*! Worse still, supposing He had found us![2]

This book is an attempt to understand better why we run away from rather than toward the God who loves us. I offer it in gratitude to my former students, friends and colleagues at the University of Dubuque Theological Seminary. My time there allowed me to gain the primary insights of this book. But above all else, I dedicate this book to my wife, Janet, who has taught me again and again the power of Christ's love best made known in another human face.

ONE

WHATEVER HAPPENED TO THE FORGIVENESS OF SINS?

It's been a long day: a senior Bible study in the morning and hospital visitation in the afternoon. The ideas are there, but the sermon is still not ready. At nearly five o'clock, you grab two commentaries to look over this evening when there is a knock at the study door. Opening it, you see Jane. Jane is very active in the congregation. She teaches Sunday school, attends the evening Bible study and rarely misses worship. Divorced nearly two years earlier, Jane is also struggling with one of the key practices of the Christian faith.

"Pastor, I know that I'm supposed to . . . I know that Jesus commanded us. But it is getting to the point that I don't even want to pray the Lord's Prayer. You know the part I mean: 'Forgive us our sins as we forgive those who sin against us.' Pastor, I want to . . . I really, really want to, but I just can't forgive my ex. Not after what he did to me and especially how he hurt the kids. I just can't forgive him." And what do you say to Jane at nearly five o'clock? Jane who desperately wants to follow Christ and yet is deeply troubled by the inconsistency between accepting forgiveness for oneself and the inability to offer that to others—what do you say to Jane?

It is very tempting to offer several replies: "Well, Jane, these things take time. You really mustn't be so hard on yourself." Or, "Jane, are you praying for him? You know it's very difficult to simultaneously pray for someone and not forgive them." Or perhaps, "Jane, I found this very disconcerting. Perhaps you should take some time off from teaching the children until your life better reflects the teachings of the church." Such responses run the usual gamut from the clichéd to the therapeutic to the judgmental. But the inadequacy of the responses is not their main problem. Their main problem is that they profoundly fail to share with Jane the heart of the Christian message. Each response assumes that Jane has the inner strength and inner resources to forgive. And each one also fails to turn Jane toward the source of forgiveness, which is not her work, but the work of the triune God.

This book is an attempt to offer an answer to Jane and to all Christians who struggle with offering faithful responses—disciple-like responses. And to begin to formulate a faithful response, we must acknowledge the changing context in which forgiveness is discussed within the church. The language of forgiveness is undergoing a dramatic change in connotation. In part, this is due to a slow but thorough loss of the language of sin among Christians. And ultimately, forgiveness will be redefined if sin talk is either muted or disappears altogether.

Cornelius Plantinga Jr. remarks on the change in our understanding of sin: "Nowadays, the accusation *you have sinned* is often said with a grin, and with a tone of that signals an inside joke."[1] To say the least, the language of sin, if used at all, sounds rather antiquated in the ears of many clergy and laity. This is often noticeable in congregational confessions of sin. You will look long and hard for the words *forgive us our sins* but they are frequently absent. Instead, multiple euphemisms rule the day. We *miscalculate, make mistakes, underestimate, overestimate, goof up, stray, trip, wander, lose our way*; but never, never under any circumstances do we actually *sin*. However, there is a deep and abiding problem with the loss of sin language and it is specifically this: Without acknowledging sin, how can there be the forgiveness of sins? And without the forgiveness of sin, how can there be salvation? Plantinga again: "For slippage in our consciousness of sin, like most fashionable follies, may be pleasant, but it is also devastating. . . . Moral beauty begins to bore us. The idea that the human race needs a Savior sounds quaint."[2]

When we lose our understanding of the magnitude of sin, we also begin to lose our appreciation for the grandeur of God's answer to sin. Miscalculations and mistakes do not need to be forgiven. For such matters, a simple reassessment of the known situation and redoubled efforts ought to suffice. But in the end, such attempts to fix ourselves seem to fall short of the goal. Such attempts frequently leave us anxious and full of questions. Why are we so shy of the language of sin?

There are a number of answers to that question, but I would begin by asking another: What part has Christian theology itself played in causing Christians to be hesitant in acknowledging sin's reality? I want to focus in this book on the way in which a different emphasis within the doctrine of the atonement might cause us to face our sin with greater honesty. And more importantly, I want to focus on how a different emphasis might cause us to face our sin with greater hope, including the hope of transformation.

It is the primary argument of this book that in order to properly understand, appropriate for oneself and offer to others forgiveness, we must begin not with human experience but with the activity of the triune God. In other words, in order to truly forgive others we must know what God the Father does through Jesus Christ the Son and how we come to appropriate that work through the power of the Holy Spirit. No other beginning point will create a suitable foundation for the power to forgive. No other place allows us to take seriously and honestly our own sin and need for forgiveness. Karl Barth states, "Only those who taste and see how gracious the Lord is can know their sin."[3] To begin with God's gracious work grants the freedom for an accurate assessment of one's condition. Christians are all too often accused of hypocrisy: denouncing the sins of others while failing to acknowledge their own. This is not the way it ought to be for people of faith. Rather, it is meant to be and can be different for Christians. Barth continues, "It is because they are held by God and cannot escape that they see that they are fleeing from Him; and it is because they are not let go and finally abandoned that they see that they are held. Known sin is always forgiven sin, known in the light of forgiveness and the triumphant grace of God."[4] To know one's sin is good news and not bad. To recognize one's alienation is to remember that God has drawn near to us. To know one's moral failure is a call to remember Jesus Christ, the only perfect one who has the power to forgive sin (Mk 2:10). Christians stand in a place of privilege in that their sin is meant to be a call to remember the God who forgives. There is no healing in the inward glance of self acceptance, but then there need not be because the God who does accept, forgive and restore has been, is and will continue to be at work.

So why do we hesitate to acknowledge our sin? As stated above, I believe that there is a great need for a new look at the doctrine of the atonement. In particular, the Western church's emphasis (since at least Anselm) on the satisfaction theory has caused us to focus primarily on our guilt. The shorthand version goes along these lines: The guilt we have accumulated as a result of our sin exacts a death penalty upon us. Jesus, who is not guilty of any sin, takes our place and dies our death. Therefore, the slate has been wiped clean and we are offered a new beginning. Thanks be to God, this is most certainly true, but what if our individual sins are not really the heart of our problem? What if it is our shame rather than our guilt that most needs to be addressed? What if our essential problem is not so much what we do or don't do, but who we are, or who we think that we are? In other words, what if our essential problem is not our failure to behave but instead our failure to recognize the truth of who God is and who we are in relationship to that God?

ASKING THE QUESTIONS IN THE PROPER ORDER

In Christian theological terms, to ask the question, whatever became of the forgiveness of sins? is to ask a question of pastoral theology. That is, we are asking a question regarding the human appropriation of or participation in God's activity. The answer to that question will be deeply influenced by the answers to two other concerns. The first concern is the *who* question. That is, who is this God at work? Second is the *what* question. What is the work of this God? Then and only then can we adequately take up the topic of the human activity of forgiveness. James Torrance writes, "From the history of Christian thought we can see that our doctrine of God determines our understanding both of the doctrine of atonement and of the nature of Christian assurance."[5] If we do not recognize who God really is, we will never be able to understand what God does; thus, we will never be able to know how to respond appropriately to this God. We will remain with our questions and our worries; we will remain with our sin.

For instance, if one begins with a concept of God that is essentially marked by a legalistic scorekeeping, we all too quickly move to the conclusion that such a God must be convinced to go contrary to his essential nature if we are to be forgiven. Such an image of God tends to generate great doubts that are manifested in one of two ways: Are we among those for whom Jesus has atoned or have we ourselves done enough to be included in the work? In this way, human beings look inward again and again to find the answer to their own forgiveness and the demand to forgive others. But such a turn inward only aggravates and reinforces our tendency to misidentify God.

But beginning with a different concept of God will yield much different results. Torrance again: "Conversely, however if our basic concept of God is that of the Triune God of grace who has being in communion as Father, Son and Holy Spirit, and who has created us to share that life of communion, then our doctrine of atonement will be seen rather as God in grace bringing these loving purposes to fulfillment in redemption."[6] The trinitarian understanding of God made known to us through Jesus Christ allows for the only place to begin in order to understand forgiveness both properly and adequately. This God does not need to be convinced to forgive; this God forgives according to his very nature at great cost to the divine life itself. This God calls human persons to look away from their own abilities, however strong or weak they may be, and trust in his work that is always prior to any human capacity or action. And the result of that looking away from the self is to place oneself on a firm foundation in which one continues to participate in God's forgiving love. This may then be experienced and acted upon as the power to forgive others.

This book seeks to ground human forgiveness in the prior work of the triune God and then and only then take up the possibilities of our accepting and offering our own forgiveness. In this way and following the excellent work of Andrew Purves, the scope of pastoral theology becomes much more closely related to systematic and historical theology. A pastoral theology of forgiveness is first the study of the ongoing work of the triune God through the participation of the church. Purves writes, "Pastoral Theology, as I intend it, is principally concerned first with the practice of God, that is, with what God does as a result of who God is. Second, it moves to reflection on the participative practice of the church within that theological perspective through our union with Christ."[7] If, as I will argue, much of our problem with forgiveness is grounded in our misidentification of God, then it is essential that we begin with a proper understanding of God. As crucial as psychology and other social sciences may be, they too prove an inadequate foundation for understanding forgiveness. And with the failure to understand God's work of forgiveness, we ultimately fail in the practice of forgiveness, be it offering it to others or accepting it for ourselves. So our emphasis will move from a focus on what the lone individual does to what God is doing. Furthermore, only when we consider the individual in community is it proper and helpful to consider the acts of accepting and offering forgiveness. The initial human context is that of the person in community; and the most important community is within the life of the triune God. Secondarily, the immediate human community to be considered is the church, the body of Jesus Christ. This expansion of the context of forgiveness is absolutely crucial in order to counteract the temptation toward the therapeutic and individualistic inward gaze.

But once this proper context is set, the conversation with social sciences and psychology in particular can be very helpful in understanding the importance of forgiveness for human thriving. The topic of forgiveness is a relatively new object of study for psychology. "In 1970, virtually no one had studied forgiveness scientifically. Forgiveness was seen as within the domain of religion. . . . Scientific study of forgiveness began in earnest only in the mid-1980s and has accelerated since that time."[8] After the 1980s, there has been an explosion of scholarly books and articles on the psychology of forgiveness. One annotated bibliography runs to well over one hundred pages.[9] In addition, there are far more popular books that utilize the discoveries of psychology on forgiveness. Forgiveness continues to be an increasingly important topic both inside and outside the church.

But there can be a downside to such popularity. Those who struggle with forgiveness may actually have their problems increased once they become aware of the physical and emotional health consequences that are associated with an incapacity or an unwillingness to forgive. Furthermore, once the topic is thought of within the field of human endeavor, Christians in particular are tempted to separate forgiveness from reconciliation, as the two are consistently separated in the psychological literature. This is a significant problem in that the Bible knows little of forgiveness separated from the restoration of relationships. "In the New Testament, while each has its nuances, forgiveness always leads to reconciliation and reconciliation results from mutual experiences of forgiveness. They cannot, finally, be separated."[10]

For that reason, in spite of the tremendous individual benefits of forgiveness (and the health problems associated with the failure to forgive), they must not be divorced from theological considerations. And yet, frequently it is the benefits of forgiveness that dominate the church's conversation, be they therapeutic or salvation centered. And so Christians face a terrible bind: we are commanded to forgive and simultaneously terrified that we lack the internal resources to do so. Once again, the answer to this dilemma is to begin with God and his activity and not the human response. In this way, we understand what James Torrance means in differentiating between the "obligations" and "conditions" of grace.[11] God's work and not ours is the crucial context for understanding forgiveness.

Because of the contemporary domination of the social science approach to the topic of forgiveness it is important to think about the relationship between psychology and theology in order to understand better how the contemporary science of forgiveness may be helpful to Christians. There are multiple models of that relationship, all of which are utilized by committed and faithful Christians.[12] However, given what I believe to be the uniqueness of the Christian understanding, I will argue from the standpoint of what is becoming known as a *Christian psychology*.[13] A Christian psychology argues that to truly understand the healing of humanity, we must first consider the reality of human nature as revealed in the Bible. Ultimately, human nature can only be understood in terms of what Karl Barth referred to as "real man."[14] "Real man" is only revealed to us in Jesus Christ. Since Chalcedon, Christians have systematically confessed Jesus Christ as truly human. He alone shows us what it means to be authentically human. But once we have begun with Christ, we will find that many of the insights of the social sciences can be properly appropriated. This I will do in chapter two.

In chapter three we will examine an insight from contemporary psychology that allows us to understand God's atoning work in a new way. This is the distinction between guilt and shame. We will see both the important distinction between the two and how the Western church's overemphasis on guilt has caused us to miss some of the key nuances of Christ's work.

With this new insight in mind, we will return to the origin story of sin contained in Genesis 3–4. Through the work of Dietrich Bonhoeffer, we will come to understand that the Bible connects sin to guilt within the context of shame. Allowing shame to become the interpretive key, we begin to gain a greater understanding of both human brokenness and God's remarkable answer to it.

Chapter five is the heart of the book. In it, we will discover the way in which God has dealt with human shame. We will first explore the atonement as a trinitarian action in which all three persons play distinctive roles in healing human shame. This will demand that we take up the second aspect of our critique. It is not simply that contemporary psychology fails to grant an adequate starting point; much of Western atonement theory has failed as well. This failure may be described as the *Latin heresy*. Having accomplished that, we will then elucidate the particular way in which Christ's crucifixion, resurrection and ascension heal our shame.

In the light of this pastoral theology, we will turn in chapter seven to the development of practices in Christian community that aid the acceptance and offering of forgiveness. Special emphasis will be placed on the importance of the confession of sins and the offering of God's forgiveness. We will see that this is done in both one-on-one situations and small group settings. Furthermore, we will explore the way in which worship allows for an ongoing appropriation of God's atoning work.

Returning to our opening scene, there is Jane, still waiting for an answer. What do we say? It is my hope that this book will aid in offering a faithful response to Jane. This will be a response that reminds Jane of God's ongoing gracious activity, helping her see that forgiveness never begins with us and that we are never alone in both our triumphs and our defeats.

TWO

COVERING OUR NAKEDNESS

Healing Through Therapy

Over forty years ago, Dr. Karl Menninger dropped a bombshell on the psychiatric world. The respected psychiatrist made a plea for the restoration of the language of sin to public discourse. Most compelling was the respected psychiatrist's attempt to remind clergy of their importance for maintaining a moral culture, a culture that recognized sin. Menninger advised,

> Clergymen have a golden opportunity to prevent some of the accumulated misapprehensions, guilt, aggressive action, and other roots of later mental suffering and mental disease. How? Preach! Tell it like it is. Say it from the pulpit. Cry it from the housetops. What shall we cry? Cry comfort, cry repentance, cry hope. Because recognition of our part in the world transgression is the only remaining hope.[1]

Although many pastors used Menninger's question in sermons, few people both in and outside the church listened. Ironically, many clergy had less hope for this approach than Menninger did. Menninger's project to address the "new morality"[2] failed because he was unable to see just how profoundly the culture had shifted. Far more had changed than simply the disappearance of the language of sin. A new priesthood of therapists had emerged and many clergy had adopted the language and worldview of that new priesthood. In Menninger's words, such clergy had a preference for the "pastoral counseling of individuals" rather than the "pulpit function" of addressing the collective life of the congregation before God.

Menninger believed in the power of clergy to address the problems of culture. But many pastors had come to believe that those problems were best analyzed through another language: the language of therapy. Many clergy had reached the conclusion that their congregations were no longer populated by "religious" people but by "psychological" people. And thus a different approach was necessary and essential. "Religious man was born to be saved; psychological man is born to be pleased. The difference was established long ago when 'I believe,' the cry of the ascetic, lost precedence to 'one feels,' the caveat of the therapeutic. And if the therapeutic is to win out, then surely the psychotherapist will be his secular spiritual guide."[3] Philip Rieff's devastating and still relevant cultural critique explains far better the loss of the language of sin.

Sin does not seem to any longer make sense because it does not conform to the new anthropology of the "psychological" person. The very goal of living has shifted away from enjoying eternity to maximizing pleasure and self-fulfillment in this life. "The therapy of all therapies is not to attach oneself exclusively to any particular therapy, so that no illusion may survive of some end beyond an intensely private sense of well-being to be generated in the living of life itself."[4] In this way, the end goal has become happiness in this life rather than salvation. Some of the best-known pastors today prove this. One only need turn on the television to behold the smiling face of Joel Osteen assuring us that we can have our *Best Life Now*! In adopting this new language, a subtle shift in traditional doctrine and practices has simultaneously occurred. There is no better illustration of this than the Christian understanding of forgiveness.

YOU ARE ACCEPTED!

One of the most famous instances of this reinterpretation occurs in Paul Tillich's famous sermon "You Are Accepted."[5] Preaching on Romans 5:20, Tillich directly tackled the problem of sin and grace, reinterpreting sin as separation from others, self and the Ground of Being.[6] In the light of that reinterpretation, grace is presented as a transformation of the self experienced as acceptance. "Do we know what it means to be struck by grace? It does *not* mean that we suddenly believe that God exists, or that Jesus is the Saviour, or that the Bible contains the truth. To believe that something *is*, is almost contrary to the meaning of grace."[7] For Tillich, doctrinal content is not only unhelpful, it actually hinders our progress in finding what we most need. And what we need most is a particular experience—a positive stroke of grace that may appear at even our darkest moments.

"Sometimes at that moment a wave of light breaks into our darkness, and it is as though a voice were saying: 'You are accepted. *You are accepted*, accepted by that which is greater than you, and the name of which you do not know. Do not ask for the name now; perhaps you will find it later.'"[8] For Tillich, our experience of acceptance is of far greater importance than knowing the name of the One who has accepted us. As long as we have the experience of acceptance, such questions may remain unanswered. Perhaps it is even better that the Acceptor remains anonymous. Knowing the name may distract us from our experience by placing further demands on our lives. "And nothing is demanded of this experience, no religious or moral or intellectual presupposition, nothing but *acceptance*."[9] Here is the transformation of a doctrine. The categories of sin and grace are now reinterpreted in terms of Carl Rogers's "client-centered" therapy.[10] Self-acceptance becomes the key to salvation, if not salvation itself.

But is "acceptance" enough? Does the experience of acceptance offer the same benefits as the experience of forgiveness? It is interesting to note that in a 2005 survey by George Barna, most Americans attested that they already feel accepted.

> Currently, nine out of ten adults (88%) feel "accepted by God." Barna listed a pair of interesting correlations related to that self-image. First, about one-third of the individuals who feel accepted by God do not consider themselves to be deeply spiritual. Second, people are twice as likely to feel accepted by God as they are to be born again—a condition that, many Protestant leaders argue, is a key reflection of God's forgiveness and ultimate acceptance.[11]

Barna's survey seems to indicate that there is a rather profound disconnection between the experience of being accepted by God and the traditional Christian understanding of living a new life in the light of that acceptance. God's acceptance of us seems completely divorced from a transformed life of discipleship. Although most Americans, Christian or otherwise, are unaware of Tillich's sermon, they seem to have embraced well his conclusion. "But sometimes it happens that we receive the power to say 'yes' to ourselves, that peace enters into us and makes us whole, that self-hate and self-contempt disappear, and that our self is reunited with itself. Then we can say that grace has come upon us."[12]

Conspicuously missing from Tillich's sermon is a personal God who is active in the world. Both sin and grace are now inner human experiences. "That is the experience of the separation of ourselves from ourselves, which is to say 'sin,' whether or not we like to use that word. Thus, the state of our whole life is estrangement from others and ourselves, because we are estranged from the Ground of our being, because we are estranged from the origin and aim of our life."[13] There seems to no longer be a need for any Acceptor outside of the individual self. The most important forgiveness is self-forgiveness. The experience of "acceptance" is far too important to be trusted to an Acceptor external to the self. And that is the heart of the problem, for ultimately, understanding the reality of God is far more important for an appropriation of forgiveness than is a good understanding of sin. The "Ground of our being" simply lacks the clarity necessary for regarding grace and the dramatic changes that it empowers.

Unfortunately, many American Christians continue to confuse acceptance with forgiveness. Furthermore, this is one of the primary reasons that many Christians struggle with forgiving others. Although important, a primary focus on one's own experience is never quite adequate to grant the capacity to forgive others. As stated above, the contemporary context is still that of the "triumph of the therapeutic." The default position is to feel one's own pain, and not nearly as often that of the other. "We've had a hundred years of analysis, and people are getting more and more sensitive, and the world is getting worse and worse. . . . What's left out is a deteriorating world. So why hasn't therapy noticed that? Because psychotherapy is only working on that 'inside' soul."[14] And so in spite of a hundred years of psychotherapy and sixty years of feeling accepted, we still are not healed.

THE UNKNOWN GOD

Ultimately, the lack of healing is directly related to the reality that the god of therapy, the god of secular acceptance is an unknown god. This god is a projection of both our desires and our fears. This god is not unlike the one Paul meets in Acts 17: "Then Paul stood in front of the Areopagus and said, 'Athenians, I see how extremely religious you are in every way. For as I went through the city and looked carefully at the objects of your worship, I found among them an altar with the inscription, "To an unknown god." What therefore you worship as unknown, this I proclaim to you'" (Acts 17:22-23).

The Athenian "unknown god" was a generic deity, a placeholder for any gods that they might have failed to include. Fearful that they might have inadvertently excluded some other divine being, the Athenians were not taking any chances. Ironically, Paul informs them that they have forgotten the only real god and so he proclaims that one, true God to them.

The Athenians, for the most part, reject Paul's identification. They prefer their god to remain unknown. They most certainly were not interested in a god who would make himself known "by a man whom he has appointed, and of this he has given assurance to all by raising him from the dead" (Acts 17:31). It is one thing to hedge one's bets. It is quite another to inadvertently blunder into the presence of the true God and therefore be required to repent because judgment is looming! In our therapeutic age, we are much like the Athenians of Acts 17. We desire a god who will heal and function as a safeguard for us. We are far less interested in one who comes, and in whose coming we are undone, even if that undoing means our salvation, our true forgiveness and acceptance. Much of contemporary Western

Christianity has been well described as "moralistic, therapeutic Deism."[15] We like our God to be a healer, but only at a distance.

FORGIVENESS IN A THERAPEUTIC CONTEXT

Forgiveness is of central importance for the Christian faith. Of all the Christian affirmations in the Apostles' Creed, it is the only doctrine that directly implies some form of reciprocation, some form of active response by the affirmers. There is not much we can do about the nature of God or the resurrection of the body. But forgiveness, that's a different matter. Two texts should suffice at this point: "Whenever you stand praying, forgive, if you have anything against anyone; so that your Father in heaven may also forgive you your trespasses" (Mk 11:25) and "Put away from you all bitterness and wrath and anger and wrangling and slander, together with all malice, and be kind to one another, tender-hearted, forgiving one another, as God in Christ has forgiven you" (Eph 4:31-32). To affirm one's belief in forgiveness implies both one's reception and one's offering of it to others. But still we struggle, sometimes with offering it and sometimes with receiving it. Into this difficulty, therapeutic forgiveness has entered.

To begin, psychologists like Everett Worthington, Steven Sandage and Robert Enright have done remarkable work in helping people who struggle with forgiveness. The work of Enright and Worthington in particular has been deeply influential in aiding therapists and their clients. They have discovered and made practical a highly accessible model to help people in offering forgiveness to others. A brief review of Enright's model will show this.

Enright's model for forgiveness involves a twenty-step process in four phases.[16] In the first phase, the client works on uncovering their anger. Here, they are encouraged to make an honest assessment of the pain they feel as a result of the thing done to them. This step is well grounded in the idea that one needs to begin where one is presently. Denying or hiding one's anger at having been hurt gets one no closer to healing. But when one has acknowledged one's true feelings about the offense, such a person now faces the opportunity to begin to move into the second phase, which involves a key decision: the decision to forgive.

"Forgiving is a choice, one you are free to make or to reject. Even if you begin you can stop the process if forgiveness seems irrelevant or too painful for you. You can take it up again when you are ready."[17] That power of choice is important in that it helps a person who has been hurt gain strength for change. It has three components: turning away from the past, looking toward the future and choosing a new way to do things. At this point the work of forgiveness has now begun.

The third phase involves the work of understanding. Here the person who has been hurt is seeking to expand their perspective, even to gain compassion for the offender. This process can ultimately lead toward giving the offender a gift, which is an attempt at a beneficent act toward the person who hurt them. The gift is the threshold for entering the final aspect of forgiveness.

As the first phase was an exploration of the negative emotion of anger, the final phase is an opportunity to discover and nurture more positive emotions. At this point, the client is invited to do the difficult work of understanding their need to forgive. That is accomplished by finding meaning in one's suffering, by finding a trusted companion with whom one may share their trouble and by finding new meaning in life. All of this is an attempt to strengthen the desire to forgive and ultimately to offer forgiveness to the offender.

Enright's model has proven helpful for many who struggle with forgiving others. In that way, it has contributed much to a therapeutic understanding of forgiveness. But there is weakness as well as strength in such an approach. As noted above, a model like Enright's that begins with human experience is never really able to transcend human experience. In spite of the moving outward of phases three and four, the key turning point remains in phase two. That is the all-important *internal* determination as to whether or not one is ready to forgive. But it is exactly at this point where many Christians struggle. For them, the question is, does the Christian who is under the mandate to forgive really have the luxury to not forgive? Everett Worthington seeks to address this problem by making a distinction between "decisional" and "emotional" forgiveness: "An individual's experience of forgiveness involves two different types of forgiveness: decisional and emotional. *Decisional forgiveness* is controlling our behavioral intentions. *Emotional forgiveness* is experiencing emotional replacement of negative unforgiving emotions with positive, other-oriented emotions."[18] Worthington also observes that there may be a significant gap between decisional and emotional forgiveness. A decision to forgive may come a good deal of time before one feels different toward the offending party.

In another place, when discussing the mandate for Christians to forgive, Worthington states, "I believe Jesus is talking about decisional forgiveness, not emotional forgiveness."[19] And he makes an even stronger theological assertion: "God *requires* decisional forgiveness of us; God *desires* emotional forgiveness."[20] These distinctions are important ones; they are meant to bring both comfort and encouragement to continue the hard work of forgiveness. Furthermore, Worthington and Enright make a strong distinction between forgiveness and reconciliation. There is most certainly a difference. One may forgive on one's own, but reconciliation takes the action of at least two parties. "Reconciliation is something God desires but does not explicitly require. Reconciliation is voluntary. . . . God does not make our reconciliation with any person sacred. Thus we do not have to reconcile."[21] In other words, God is for reconciliation but it is by no means mandatory.

That is a very strong statement and ultimately an extremely difficult one to reconcile with the New Testament. First, there are the rather straightforward commands of Jesus: "So when you are offering your gift at the altar, if you remember that your brother or sister has something against you, leave your gift there before the altar and go; first be reconciled to your brother or sister, and then come and offer your gift" (Mt 5:23-24). Jesus seems to make little provision there for choosing when and if his followers will reconcile with those from whom they are alienated.

Second, to draw too bright a line between forgiveness and reconciliation is to take forgiveness out of its larger context. Individual acts of forgiveness always presume the greater work of reconciliation which has already occurred through the agency of the triune God.

> From now on, therefore, we regard no one from a human point of view; even though we once knew Christ from a human point of view, we know him no longer in that way. So if anyone is in Christ, there is a new creation: everything old has passed away; see, everything has become new! All this is from God, who reconciled us to himself through Christ, and has given us the ministry of reconciliation; that is, in Christ God was reconciling the world to himself, not counting their trespasses against them, and entrusting the message of reconciliation to us. (2 Cor 5:16-19)

Human forgiveness occurs in the ongoing pursuit of reconciliation, which is what Paul refers to as a "ministry of reconciliation." Arguing with the authority of the New Testament in mind, it is difficult to imagine individual acts of forgiveness separate from the context of reconciliation.[22]

The final problem in separating forgiveness from reconciliation is what it says about one's anthropology. As a Christian, Worthington certainly acknowledges God as Father, Son and Holy Spirit. Furthermore, he also acknowledges that human beings "mirror" the triune God.[23] We are created for relationships, but we struggle because of sin. At the same time, however, Worthington's understanding of human anthropology is problematic because his understanding of the Trinity appears to be insufficient. "God is three beings in continual interaction within the Trinity."[24] Over the centuries, the church has explicitly taught that God is not three separate beings in continuous interaction with one another. Instead, God is one being in three persons. There is no divisibility into separate beings, but God is, always and only, Father, Son and Holy Spirit.

Precision in language is crucial for many reasons. For our purposes here, it is to determine the meaning of *imago Dei*. If we do believe that we bear the image of the triune God, than how we understand the Trinity will determine how we understand ourselves. If God is "three beings in continual interaction" then it is adequate to maintain that we are created "for" relationships. On the other hand, if God is one who is Father, Son and Holy Spirit, then that means that relationship is tantamount to identity. There is no way for us to know or understand the Christian God outside of who God is as Father, Son and Holy Spirit. This means that ultimately there is no way to understand ourselves absent of relationships. But that is exactly the human dilemma. We see relationships as important but not essential. Identity is somehow something that we are in ourselves apart from anyone else and therefore we can enter and depart relationships as we see fit. No doubt that is how we function. The question is this: Is that really who we are and does that ever lead us closer to God and neighbor? Our self-understanding and our understanding of God have a deep and profound connection. To get one of those wrong will always lead to an obscuring of the other. Furthermore, as we will see in the next chapters, we do not understand ourselves well enough to understand God without some form of intervention, that is, without God's self-revelation.

None of the above is meant to question Worthington's faith or the good work that he has done. Instead, it is only to seek and to inquire about the theological basis for some of his assertions. His focus on individual identity over relational identity necessarily places emphasis upon what the individual can do by themselves. The power to decide is crucial. We decide when to forgive and we decide when to reconcile. Somehow, we will just know when it is appropriate to do one or the other of those based upon our individual needs.[25]

THE CENTRAL PROBLEM

But what if that is exactly our central problem? What if we do not really know our individual needs because we do not know ourselves or are afraid to know ourselves? What if left to ourselves, we will never find it an appropriate time to forgive or to reconcile? What if our sin has not only alienated us from God and neighbor but has also alienated us from ourselves, including our self-understanding? What if sin in essence is actually the quest for identity separate from our relationship to God and neighbor? But to undertake that quest leads us

back to the *unknown god* of contemporary therapy who ultimately is the projection of both our fears and desires.

Does this mean that there is nothing for Christians to learn
from contemporary psychological models? Of course that is not
the case. At the same time, however, it does mean that we must
be more skeptical about our perceptions of both God and ourselves if we would gain true insights from the social sciences.

Christian psychologist Eric Johnson writes, "The so-called
noetic effects of sin . . . lead to misunderstandings regarding
reality so serious that they obscure our interpretations and warp
our descriptions of important aspects of God and his creation."[26]
The "noetic effects" of sin refer to the reality that our brokenness
extends to our powers of perception. We do not accurately perceive reality. And the closer that we get to the "big questions,"
the more likely it is that we will misinterpret what we perceive.
To say it another way, creation is silent at the very point where
we require a definitive word. Our powers of observation fail us
when and where we need them the most. We live in a wonderful
world full of remarkable things, but it simply does not provide
us with the key to understanding the one true thing that can
unlock the greatest mysteries. In other words, it cannot help us
recognize the gracious nature of the Creator.

Reflecting on Genesis 3:8 ("They heard the sound of the LORD
God walking in the garden at the time of the evening breeze, and
the man and his wife hid themselves from the presence of the
LORD God among the trees of the garden"), Ray Anderson makes
two important points. First, "there never was a time when
humans were solely dependent on the impersonal, created world
to expound the nature and purpose of God."[27] That is, God does
not and never has left us alone in our ignorance, but comes to us
and reveals his very self to us. God seeks to make himself known

to us because he loves us. And second, the verse also reveals our human tendency to run and hide from the very God who graciously and personally comes to us. We are not abandoned to our broken powers of observation, but our broken powers of observation make us fearful of the very answers we might discover. We hide from the God who approaches not because of who he actually is, but because of who we fear him to be.

THE CONSCIENCE

Perhaps the primary example of our broken powers of perception that fail us where we need them the most is the human conscience. This internal compass of right and wrong would seem to be the most important way of knowing when to forgive and when to reconcile. But is it trustworthy? Even after we have named our pain and identified our anger, can we still be certain that we have an adequate place to make such an important decision?

At best, the human conscience in biblical terms is fallible. It does not provide us with true knowledge of God, or of our relationship to God. And it most certainly is not the pure voice of the Holy Spirit whispering in our ear. A few scriptural references readily show the ambiguous nature of conscience.

Sometimes the conscience is weak, as in 1 Corinthians 8:7: "It is not everyone, however, who has this knowledge. Since some have become so accustomed to idols until now, they still think of the food they eat as food offered to an idol; and their conscience, being weak, is defiled." Sometimes the conscience offers a clear and consistent affirmation of God's work: "I am speaking the truth in Christ—I am not lying; my conscience confirms it by the Holy Spirit" (Rom 9:1). And sometimes the conscience lies: "To the pure all things are pure, but to the corrupt and unbelieving nothing is pure. Their very minds and consciences are corrupted" (Tit 1:15). To reiterate, the conscience is not the most accurate of human faculties. This arbitrator of moral judgment is by no means an infallible guide for Christian thought and behavior. In the next chapters, we will examine one possible explanation for the origin of conscience. Furthermore, we will look at the way in which conscience fails to understand guilt adequately.

THE PRIMACY OF FORGIVENESS

As we have seen, there can be little doubt that the therapeutic understanding of forgiveness has dominated the contemporary conversation. This is due in part to therapy's practical aspect. Forgiveness is obviously good because it works. Both those who offer forgiveness and those who receive forgiveness are helped. Who can be against forgiveness when it is so obviously effective? But Fraser Watts offers a word of caution regarding the pragmatic feature of forgiveness: "This widening of the practice of forgiveness is undoubtedly to be welcomed, and I have no concerns about forgiveness being practiced outside an explicitly religious context. However, the question is whether something important is not lost by approaching forgiveness in such a narrowly pragmatic spirit."[28] What may be lost in our pragmatic context is true forgiveness, that is, forgiveness that may be a cause for suffering rather than immediate fulfillment.[29] We dare not underestimate the consumer mindset of our context. Good choices like good purchases must make fairly immediate sense to us. With a primarily pragmatic frame of mind (forgiveness is good because it is helpful) we would view forgiveness as akin to other goods. We like forgiveness because we find it helpful, much like a two-week vacation.

Perhaps the greatest failure of the therapeutic understanding is that it sees everything within the dominant context of better functioning. Forgiveness is important insofar as the failure to forgive (and in particular the failure to practice emotional forgiveness) leads to poor health and emotional problems. But Christians must question that larger context of the forgiveness/healing relationship. In biblical terms, the priority is reversed. Healing is understood within the far greater arena of God's forgiving (i.e., atoning/reconciling) work. The story of the healing of the paralytic in Mark 2:1-12 reveals a new dimension of Jesus' ministry. He has power not only to heal (as demonstrated a number of times in Mk 1) but also to forgive.

In this passage, it is important to understand and take note of the two distinct works that Christ performs. Jesus both forgives and heals the paralyzed man. "'Which is easier, to say to the paralytic, "Your sins are forgiven," or to say, "Stand up and take your mat and walk"? But so that you may know that the Son of Man has authority on earth to forgive sins'—he said to the paralytic—'I say to you, stand up, take your mat and go to your home'" (Mk 2:9-11). Furthermore, it is essential to pay attention to the order of the two works and the time break between them. What Mark 2 can help us see is that there truly is a profound relationship between forgiveness and healing. In some ways, this healing is a rather humorous event in the early ministry of Jesus. One must wonder what the homeowner thought as he witnessed the roof of his home being torn open so that the paralytic might be brought into Jesus' presence! In addition, one must wonder what the paralytic and his friends thought when in response, Jesus pronounces him to be forgiven of his sins, rather than tending to the obvious health concerns of the man. One wonders if the man and his friends were tempted to say, "Well thank you very much but as you may have noticed, we did have one other concern!" But this, of course, is no failure in empathy or concern on Jesus' part. Instead, we must pay attention to how this event establishes the priority of forgiveness in the ministry of Christ. Commenting on this text, T. F. Torrance notes how this miracle reveals not only Jesus' power, but the way in which he manifests it. "Jesus took care in His preaching never to give a compelling manifestation of Himself, lest by an open display of His majesty and might He might crush men to the ground, leaving no room for faith or repentance or decision."[30] The reason for this is that the end of history has dawned in him. Without creating a safe space for response, we would be overwhelmed by the sheer majesty of God's entrance into our reality, into history. And so, "Jesus deliberately held the Word and its action apart in order to leave room for repentance and faith, but at the same time He followed up the Word with a sign which gave ample evidence of His saving power."[31] Not only does Jesus save, he also creates a place for us in which we may respond to his overthrowing of human sin. This is accomplished by leaving a gap between our forgiveness and our healing. "It was precisely that lapse of time or eschatological reserve between the Word of the Kingdom and its power that Jesus was concerned to preserve in His *kerygma*."[32]

Torrance's key insight is that the word of forgiveness is where we must begin because it is what we need prior to any healing. The word of forgiveness precedes even any human understanding of need or preparation. Just the reverse of what we normally think, it is Christ's prior act of forgiveness that gives us a place to be before him. As Torrance has it, forgiveness has priority because none of us could stand before Jesus in the full manifestation of his power. It must necessarily come first because forgiveness is essential in preparing us for any further manifestation of God's power. Without being first forgiven, we would be undone before him. Torrance again: "The Church lives between these two moments, between the Cross and the *parousia*, between the Word of forgiveness and the final act of healing, between Pentecost and the resurrection of the body. In the mercy of God the Word of the Gospel and the final deed of God are partially held apart in eschatological reserve until the *parousia*."[33]

By means of the *eschatological reserve*, Christ intends to leave space for response. Therefore, our appropriate response to forgiveness is repentance and the decision to live life in a new way. That of course is the opposite of what many Christians think. For many, the tendency is to first feel sorry for our sins and then to ask for forgiveness. But that is not God's procedure. This new way has already broken into human reality in the person and work of Jesus Christ. Those who have accepted this forgiveness are empowered by the Holy Spirit to begin to experience the realities of the age to come even in this present fallen age. In other words, forgiveness is a certainty because this is the central manifestation of Christ's power. In the presence of Jesus, one need never doubt that sin is forgiven because of some deficit in oneself. What we do not have the power to accomplish, God has already done in Christ. Yet how one experiences this forgiveness is not certain. The secondary work of healing, prior to Christ's full manifestation in the eschaton, is not yet total. There are signs of healing even as there are signs of reconciliation that point us toward the close of the age in which we will fully realize that Christ is all in all (Col 3:11). Awaiting that, even though not all bodies are healed nor all relationships reconciled, one need not despair that Jesus has authority to (and has indeed) decisively address human sin through its forgiveness.[34]

At the same time, Mark 2 illustrates that Christ is not merely interested in the pronouncement of the forgiveness of human guilt, but is desirous of the transformation of the status of human beings. Christ desires to give forgiven humans a new identity that is the restored son/daughter relationship to his Father. As we shall see below, in this way, not only is the guilt of sin addressed (it is forgiven!) but the shame of sin is also taken on (it is healed through the gift of a new identity).

"Garments of Skin"—the Role of Therapy

In spite of the difficulties presented by a therapy that does not begin with revelation, that is, alienated from a true knowledge of the human self, can there be a positive and independent role for the therapeutic project? The New Testament, of course, is full of examples of healing extended to those who do not recognize Jesus as Lord. Actually, the Gospels seem to offer only stories of healing that are not dependent on recognition of Jesus' identity.[35] Therefore, the priority of forgiveness does not mean that that no healing may occur until one recognizes one's forgiveness. God is gracious; God is loving and of course does not wait for us. Our concern up to this point has only been insisting that forgiveness is God's work ever and always before it may be ours. Even more explicitly, forgiveness is ever and always the work of the triune God into which we are invited to participate.

How then, might one describe a positive role for therapy absent an understanding of God's unique work? Genesis 3:21 offers a helpful metaphor: "And the LORD God made garments of skins for the man and for his wife, and clothed them." Dietrich Bonhoeffer offers this commentary: "'He made them cloaks,' says the Bible. That means that God accepts human beings for what they are, as fallen creatures. . . . God's new action with humankind is to uphold and preserve humankind in its fallen world, in its fallen orders, for death—for the resurrection, for the new creation, for Christ."[36]

The work of cloaking is a good work; but simultaneously it is an incomplete one. Therapy is a participation in God's good work, but it is a penultimate one. Even at its most successful, it points beyond itself toward a greater culmination, a more complete healing. God graciously clothes, mercifully offers help to all in the midst of their brokenness. But still, it remains an aspect of healing without the fulfillment or sufficiency of the promised reconciliation (Gen 3:15) that remains yet to come. Without its theological basis, therapy is an attempt to deal with symptomatic behavior, bringing some relief without dealing with the root issue. The tragic nature of the therapeutic (like all pagan science) is at its best it is only able to provide a better set of clothes to wear on the way to one's funeral! At least Freud understood this as the best goal of therapy: "No doubt fate would find it easier than I do to relieve you of your illness. But you will be able to convince yourself that much will be gained if we succeed in transforming your hysterical misery into common unhappiness."[37] Any therapy that would promise more is in danger of becoming a new religion, a new path of salvation.

So how does a Christian participate in this preliminary work? I would affirm its helpfulness as an act of common grace, available to everyone regardless of their faith, or lack thereof. Just as with Adam and Eve, therapy is an act of mercy that may be extended to all in the midst of their sin. Is it permissible for it to be done without reference to our new understanding of putting on the Lord Jesus Christ without making provision for the flesh (Rom 13:14)? It is very important for the Christian therapist to be respectful regarding the faith (or its lack) of anyone they might encounter. Such respect reflects the humble nature of the God we serve who does not demand recognition, let alone worship, prior to acting on our behalf. Therefore, such care may and ought to be offered to all. At the same time, as appropriate, the covering may be offered in the light of the fullness of our being clothed in Jesus Christ. That is, there can be an interpretation of the therapeutic act that understands itself as an act of mercy on the road to something other than inevitable death—it is grace, a foretaste of what will come in power when the fall is reversed by God's descent in the incarnation (Phil 3:5-6). This is the grand reversal of the Son's fall (which is an intentional descent), of the Son's nakedness and shaming that does not merely cover our own shame but heals it. It is the story of the human being, the new Adam, who does not run from the Father but rather embraces his will; who drains the dregs of the cup, and who is sold that we might be redeemed.

THREE

GUILT AND SHAME

In chapter two we discussed the incomplete work of therapy by means of an analogy from Genesis 3 wherein God mercifully clothes Adam and Eve. One may argue that modern psychology is unable to address fully the human predicament in that it lacks the revealed truth of Scripture—it has no direct access to the depths of the human problem (in Christian terms, sin) because it has no access to the full reality of what it means to be human. We are bearers of God's image (Gen 1:26); that is, we are created to share in and be stewards of the Creator's glory. Lacking this revealed understanding, secular psychology cannot fully explain either the heights of human nobility or the depths of human degradation. Furthermore, following the Christian orthodox tradition, we may affirm that Jesus Christ alone fully reveals to us not only who God is, but also what true humanity is. To affirm Christ's full humanity means, in part, that Jesus alone may reveal to us what is healthy human functioning. He alone is completely developed and psychologically whole. Is there a way to bridge the gap between what theology and psychology may teach us? To that possibility we now turn.

THE PHENOMENA OF THE HUMAN

Karl Barth offers a way forward in his masterful theological anthropology.[1] In *Church Dogmatics* III/2 he speaks of the "phenomena of the human"[2] that we are able to observe. The problem of such phenomena is their inability to offer the objective standard of true or real humanity. Although it may seem counterintuitive, we really cannot understand human behavior, let alone human nature, by observation of the human person. At best, we are only able to discover what Barth referred to as "symptoms of the human." The observation of human behavior poses a puzzle without a key to unlock it. For Barth, true humanity can only be discovered in Jesus Christ. To begin any place else fails to adequately address both the degradation and the glory of humanity, and ultimately leads to human despair in that one is always left without proper direction in understanding oneself or one's neighbor.

Barth, of course, has been often critiqued for his fideism, that is, his affirmation of a basis for knowledge that is dependent on a prior commitment of faith. Many have argued both for and against Barth on this issue. The scope of this book does not allow for either a rehearsal or refutation of those charges. What I desire to do here is to remind us that Barth is certain that just because knowledge of the truly human begins with Jesus Christ does not mean that it ends there. Once one has discovered true humanity in Jesus, the other categories (for example, sociology and psychology) prove to be useful, after all. Their utility reemerges once they find their proper ordering. "We are now in a position to see them not merely as phenomena but to estimate them as real indications of the human. . . . We can now grant that all human self-knowledge, even though it be autonomous, is justifiable to the extent that, according to what we have learned from the Word and revelation of God, it is not pursuing a will-o'-the-wisp in its investigation of man."[3]

Christians have historically affirmed that Jesus Christ is both fully God and fully human. It is the fullness of his humanity with which we begin if we are to observe true human nature. He becomes the objective standard by which all other observable human phenomena may be understood. But the problem, as we have already observed in chapter two, is not a lack of information. We have more than enough data to explore. But where does one begin? Barth was certain that beginning with the observation of human behavior in general or a philosophical understanding of an abstract human nature will not yield for us what we most need: an answer to our problem. It is quite impossible for us to "jump out of our skin" in order to independently observe or hypothesize a pristine human nature. Barth would maintain that although we cannot do that, we do not despair, because God has not left us alone in our ignorance. Instead, the triune God has actively engaged the world and revealed to us the true reality of humanity in the person of Jesus of Nazareth.

Our primary interest remains a pastoral one. In this book we are not particularly concerned with epistemological questions (How do we know what we know?). Instead in this chapter we want to consider how important it is for our healing that Jesus Christ alone simultaneously reveals both the true face of God and the true human face. Our concern remains to plumb the depths of our forgiveness and to know that the triune God has sufficiently answered our problems and the cries of the human heart.

Therefore, acknowledging the triumph of God's grace and the necessity of focusing on what God does, we may now better explore the fuller implications of what has been accomplished for us. Once again accepting the reality that Jesus Christ is both our starting and ending point, we may now faithfully explore what the phenomena of the human tell us of human nature and its associated problems. Beginning with the fullness of humanity revealed in Jesus, we may now better understand the brokenness that is revealed in all humans.

THE SHAME/GUILT DISTINCTION

There is one particular "phenomenon of the human" to which we must now turn our attention. This particular insight gained from contemporary psychology will grant us a fuller perspective of human nature even as we continue to grant the triune God the privileged position of self-revelation; it can help us better explore the realities of what we can only adequately learn through Jesus of Nazareth. Here we may now better explore the way in which God has not only healed human guilt but also human shame. This shame/guilt distinction, when read in the light of God's revelation, should cause us to go back and reassess earlier attempts to understand adequately the depth and breadth of our salvation.

There is a very important distinction that may be made between guilt and shame and the way in which they are experienced. We will examine both and see how both relate to the problem of human sin. Because of the Western church's emphasis on the penal substitution model of the atonement, the experience of guilt has dominated Christian circles.[4] One often hears of Catholic guilt, Lutheran guilt, Calvinist guilt, Baptist guilt and so on. There is plenty of guilt to go around in the Western church. Many Christians struggle mightily with sinful things that they have done or good things that they have left undone. It is not a happy experience and is often referenced by both those Christians who have remained in the church and, even more interestingly, by those Christians who no longer associate with formal Christian communities.[5]

DIFFERENT TYPES OF GUILT

It can be said that guilt has both an objective and a subjective dimension. That means that guilt can refer either to the state of having done something wrong or to the emotion of feeling oneself to be in the wrong. The great Jewish philosopher Martin Buber delineated three types of guilt.[6] First, there is *civil* guilt. This is the objective state of a person in terms of society's laws. An example of this is when you receive a speeding ticket and you pay it. In doing so, you have pled "guilty." The court accepts that plea as well as the money that you submit to atone for your violation.

The second type of guilt that Buber cites is *existential-religious* guilt. Like civil guilt, this too describes an objective state. This type takes up a much larger area of human experience because, of course, even though almost all crimes would be considered sinful, there are plenty of sins that are not crimes. Here we are considering anything that might cause a breach in a relationship with another person, whether that is God, another person or oneself. This is what we most often mean when we refer to someone as a sinner.

Finally, in Buber's terms, there is *psychologic* guilt. Such guilt refers to the subjective experience of feeling guilty. This is the internal dimension of guilt that may or may not be related to objective guilt. In other words, a person can feel guilty when they have committed a crime (category one) or a sin (category two), which are the objective realms. On the other hand, it is also possible to experience psychologic guilt whether or not one is objectively guilty. This distinction is a very important one for most people dealing with problems of forgiveness. It often relates to the problem that some people face when they find themselves unable to forgive themselves.

The subjective world of guilt may be described in terms of a number of feelings and experiences. These include a sense of debt, or feelings of transgression or trespassing. Note how those first two take in the two traditional ways in which the Lord's Prayer refers to human sinning.[7] The liturgical language of the church has intuitively known that *sin* needs further elucidation at the subjective level. Thus, both traditional renderings of the prayer, be it *trespasses* or *debts*, are, in a certain way, superior to the more *accurate* translation of *sin*. The subjective state of owing what cannot be repaid or committing an offense that cannot be undone more accurately represents our subjective sinful state. Other terms associated with guilt include doing injury, not taking responsibility, feeling failure to uphold duty or obligation. Finally, guilt relates to committing offenses, culpability, being wrong, good or bad.[8] One can say that the spectrum of guilt runs along the scale of degrees of badness: the guiltier a person is, the worse they are. We will see below how that scale is very different from the measurement of shame.

The Bible represents guilt in a number of ways.[9] It should not be surprising that since the Old Testament tells the story of the nation of Israel, a strong sense of corporate responsibility is emphasized. Guilt tends to be attached to groups of people. At the same time, it is certainly the case that individuals can bring guilt upon a whole group. Examples of this include Genesis 26:10, Deuteronomy 24:4 and, perhaps most frightening to us, Joshua 7, which relates the story of Achan. In this passage we see that the guilt due to the disobedience of one person falls upon the nation as a whole. The guilt is only lifted when Achan, along with his family, animals and goods are stoned (Josh 7:24-25).

With the prophets, however, there begins a growing emphasis on individual guilt (although corporate guilt certainly remains) and personal responsibility. Example passages include Micah 6:6-8, and most famously Jeremiah 31:29-30, in which it becomes clear that in the future, God will hold each person accountable for their own actions. No longer will the sins of one be attributed to the larger group: "In those days they shall no longer say: 'The parents have eaten sour grapes, and the children's teeth are set on edge.' But all shall die for their own sins; the teeth of everyone who eats sour grapes shall be set on edge."

Still, it is the New Testament that most clearly emphasizes the idea of personal responsibility. Each person stands individually accountable to God. Furthermore, sinful behavior is complicated in that a person is accountable not simply for their outward acts but also for the inner motivations. "You have heard that it was said to those of ancient times, 'You shall not murder'; and 'whoever murders shall be liable to judgment.' But I say to you that if you are angry with a brother or sister, you will be liable to judgment; and if you insult a brother or sister, you will be liable to the council; and if you say, 'You fool,' you will be liable to the hell of fire" (Mt 5:21-22). Jesus' Sermon on the Mount marks a profound change in that not only particular bad deeds, but also individual motivations and attitudes are now understood to be equally sinful and liable for judgment.

At the same time, the New Testament marks a *universalization* of guilt. All people, Jew and Gentile alike, are culpable. Paul emphasizes this in Romans 1:18–3:20. "What then? Are we any better off? No, not at all; for we have already charged that all, both Jews and Greeks, are under the power of sin" (Rom 3:9).

The entire human race stands guilty before God. All individuals, nations and tribes are judged unrighteous and accountable.

THE SUBJECTIVE NATURE OF GUILT

We examined in the last chapter the ways in which therapeutic categories often replace the traditional discussions of sin and its forgiveness. One of the primary reasons for this is the modern focus on the subjective experience of what Christianity names as sin. The Bible's sole focus on guilt is its objective status. It is a legal or judicial category. It does not refer to any subjective experience of guilt. On the other hand, psychology has tended to view guilt as a problem giving rise to neurosis. Furthermore it has tended to focus on the inner dynamics of guilt (the feelings) rather than on the objective nature. Sigmund Freud associated guilt with a type of inner anxiety.[10] In his opinion such anxiety arises from an internal conflict between constitutive elements of the psyche in the basic developmental process. Prior to age three to four, Freud believed, children do not experience feelings of guilt. They may be ashamed or fear punishment, but do not yet have the experience of guilt. That comes sometime between the ages of three to six, when the superego emerges. In Freudian terms, the superego develops as a child begins to identify with a parent or parental figure.

Internalizing this desire to please another, the child begins to develop both an ego ideal (this is what it means to be a good human being) and a conscience (don't do that!). Furthermore, guilt tends to generate all sorts of problems because of the other complicated dynamics that are occurring at this point of the developmental stage. The child both loves and hates the parent as the principal authority figure,[11] and for Freud, that is more than enough to explain neurosis generated by guilt.

Resulting problems can include self-hatred, low self-esteem, severely ascetic behaviors and addictions.

Of course, like in most things, the field of psychology has progressed far beyond Freud in the study of guilt. We will discuss that below when we begin to unpack the important differences between guilt and shame. In examining Christian care issues, one can observe that the key element for Christian caregivers regarding guilt is the reality that a person can be guilty without feeling guilty, as well as the obverse of that: a person can feel guilty without actually being guilty. In theological terms many guilt feelings are normal. They are an appropriate response to the objective reality of guilt. As a matter of fact, normal guilt feelings can be seen as a part of God's gracious response to us. If we do something bad we feel bad; if we willfully fail to do the right thing, we will feel a sense of failure. Not unlike the physical pain response, guilt feelings can be gracious checks on certain behaviors. They are warnings to turn back, to cease and desist, or to go back and try a different approach.

At the same time, however, there are also inappropriate guilt feelings. People can cling to feelings of guilt long past having sought forgiveness. They can also heighten the feelings wherein the (self-) punishment simply does not fit the crime. A very important part of Christian caring is helping people sort through some of these feelings, claiming normal guilt and letting go of inappropriate guilt feelings. We will examine in chapter seven some ways to sort through those issues in terms of the confession of one's sins.

Freud did very little to distinguish any difference between shame and guilt. This, one might say, is a real "shame," for it has probably created a multitude of problems in the last century. Chief of these is the reinforcement of Freud's famous prejudice regarding religion. Feelings of guilt (either subjective or objective) tended to be viewed as problematic and often led to deeper psychological disorders. Thus religion, be it Christianity or any other that spoke of sin and its judgment, would come to be understood as the fount of many problems. If Christianity causes one to feel guilty and feeling guilty leads to poor human functioning, there must be something wrong with Christianity, the reasoning goes.

Of course, there have been plenty of abuses of Christian teaching. Unfortunately, many sermons, Sunday school classes and so on have aided and abetted a false sense of guilt in some people. Too much moralization posing as gospel proclamation has done great harm and thus has been rejected in our post-Christendom era. Indeed some aspects of Christianity have majored in the minors, giving too much importance to cultural differences (e.g., dancing, card playing and drinking). Furthermore, the rejection of the church's penchant for moralizing on such small matters has helped lead to a major change in what once were considered moral absolutes. The church's traditional teaching on far more important matters (issues of sexuality, the use of money and so on) are now also viewed with suspicion. In reaction to a sense of false guilt many would consider most judgments of whether something is moral or immoral to be highly subjective. If it feels right to you (i.e., you don't feel guilty) than it probably is all right for you. At the same time, it is unfair and most unhelpful to issue a blanket condemnation of objective guilt because of poor teaching. The post-Christendom church has a tremendous opportunity to own its past failures while maintaining a doctrine of sin that will help people to live in ways that lead to loving God, neighbor and oneself.

THE PROBLEM OF CONSCIENCE

Once again, good pastoral care ought to help us navigate between true and false feelings of guilt. We need the help of one another to do this because left to ourselves we do not have an objective standard regarding false feelings of guilt. The human conscience is not a reliable arbitrator for distinguishing false from true guilt. Bruce Narramore's *No Condemnation* is a classic study of how the conscience is and is not helpful.[12] Narramore is partially dependent on Dietrich Bonhoeffer's thought for understanding the origin of the human conscience, which we will examine in greater detail in the next chapter. In part, what Narramore seeks to do is to answer modern psychological theories that tend to expect either too little or too much from the conscience.[13] His primary concern is how to determine when guilt feelings are or are not appropriate. Where is the line between appropriate guilt for having done something wrong and neurotic self-condemnation? In general terms, the line is crossed when a person condemns themselves rather than their behavior.

A major part of the problem occurs in confusing rejection and correction. "Just as the Scriptures reveal a resource for a positive sense of self-esteem, they also make it clear that fears of punishment and rejection have no place in Christian motivation. There is a place for divine correction (chastisement), remorse, and repentance. But these are distinct from threats of punishment and rejection."[14]

God's correction has a future orientation, modifying our behavior in order to live in harmony with God and neighbor. Its focus on behavior allows the chastised person to focus on what has been done wrong in the past in order to make better decisions for the future. Chastisement implies behavior modification within a loving relationship that will make for better future living. Such correction is meant to inspire hope. On the other hand, punishment as Narramore distinguishes here implies a more global judgment. Its focus on past sin and failure tends to cut off the punished person from any future relationship. Punishment in this sense feels like rejection and so it inspires despair.

There are four inadequate responses to the guilt feelings that arise from a sense of rejection.[15] First, one may *give in* and suffer self-punishment that is accompanied by a loss of self esteem. Such a response leads to depression and deepening anxiety. The person who *gives in* concludes, "I'm just not a very good person." A second response is to *rationalize* or attempt to *hide* from the guilt feelings. Such a person may conclude, "I may be bad, but I'm not the only one." Or, "there are plenty of people who are worse than I am." Such a flight from personal responsibility may end up making it difficult for a person to distinguish true from false guilt.

A third response is to *rebel*. This can be done either actively or passively. In active fashion, it may be observed in people who grew up in the church but quit participating because of the accumulated guilt feelings.[16] In attempting to throw off the bad feelings, they frequently throw off the faith as well. This may, in part, explain the vitriol with which some former Christians attack the church. They are angry because of how they were made to feel, and apparently still do feel. The passive form of rebellion may be observed in believers who simply go through the motions. They have given up on active service because they feel defeated; fearing further failure, they stop trying. They do not actively strike out against the faith, but they have no joy in it either. It is a burden that cannot be shrugged. The final guilt response is *to confess and alter one's behavior*. At first this might seem like a positive response, but in reality, it is doomed to failure. This type of response is an effort at self-atonement. It is the Sisyphean labor of working at a task that can never be accomplished. All such attempts end in the same way: frustration and despair.

What Narramore offers to these ineffective responses is a way to help move away from the condemning conscience toward a more constructive and faithful understanding of one's experience. It must be emphasized again how conscience is an insufficient guide to reality. Its voice is not to be trusted because it remains too subjective. Alone, the conscience does not maintain a true and faithful vision of reality. It must be transformed by the Word of God. Then and only then can it become useful for leading a person toward a godly or constructive sorrow for real guilt, for the ways in which one has truly not followed Christ. Narramore states that this sorrow is "love-motivated emotion closely related to guilt feelings yet radically different. Whereas psychological guilt is a self-punitive process, constructive sorrow is a love-motivated desire to change that is rooted in concern for others."[17] The key to interpretation is the origin point of the feeling: is it self- or other focused? As we will see in the next chapter, our foreparents, Adam and Eve, were motivated by self-preservation.

Finally, Narramore's work helps us understand how new breakthroughs in the social sciences can inform a theological conversation. As helpful as his work is, it predates a very important distinction between guilt and shame. Much of what Narramore describes as guilt motivation would now be discussed under the general heading of shame.

Beyond the church's role in creating false guilt may lay a far greater problem: participation in the shaming of people. If false guilt (What you did was wrong!) has caused some to walk away from the church, shaming (You are a bad person!) has done far greater damage. It can be argued that the cultural moral shift that the West has undergone in the last century has had far more to do with the categories of shame than of guilt. And it is the topic of shame to which we now turn.

SHAME

The discussion of shame in the Bible is a much more complicated matter. Guilt is understood to be an objective category regarding a person's standing in relationship to others, but shame is a far more subjective phenomenon. Furthermore, in the two Testaments the presentation of shame differs greatly. The Old Testament references shame well over one hundred times.[18] Shame is primarily discussed in the Psalms and the prophetic books, particularly Jeremiah, Isaiah and Ezekiel. Those references are often pleas that the people not come to shame and warnings that as a result of sin they will. Idolatry is most often associated with shame. Isaiah 45:16 typifies the usage: "All of them are put to shame and confounded, the makers of idols go in confusion together." At the same time, shame is portrayed in a positive light and may actually function as a sign of hope. The presence of shame represents the possibility of repentance. Without shame, however, the people are likely to continue on their path to destruction. Jeremiah 8:12: "They acted shamefully, they committed abomination; yet they were not at all ashamed, they did not know how to blush. Therefore they shall fall among those who fall; at the time when I punish them, they shall be overthrown, says the LORD." Here we see clearly the distinction between objective and subjective shame. The people are acting shamefully in their sinful disobedience but have lost the subjective feelings of shame. The people truly are lost when they no longer are embarrassed by their sin.

Turning to the Christian tradition, this positive aspect of shame was emphasized in the sixteenth century by some of the Reformers as the "first" and "second" uses of the law.[19] In the first case, a person might feel a sense of shame in contemplating a particular sinful act (theft, for example). Insofar as shame may help prevent egregious acts of sin, it participates in the restraining of human depravity. Regarding the second use, shame has the potential to reveal humanity's brokenness and desperate need for God. It does not save but it can help a person understand that they are lost, or at the very least that something is terribly wrong. One might then ask, "Does this mean that God directly sends shame?" My opinion would be that the answer to that question is *no*. However, it may well mean that we should not be surprised that we experience discomfort (and at times, profound discomfort) when we go against the "grain of the universe." Furthermore, when shame does have positive aspects, it is an illustration of the way that God is able to work good in all circumstances (Rom 8:28).

Turning to the New Testament, one learns that shame occupies a much less prominent place. The negative sense of shame (*aischynē*) occurs only about thirty times. The prominent understanding of shame can be seen in Hebrews 12:2: "Looking to Jesus the pioneer and perfecter of our faith, who for the sake of the joy that was set before him endured the cross, disregarding its *shame*, and has taken his seat at the right hand of the throne of God." The meaning of this is made explicit in 1 Corinthians 1:18-31, where it can be seen that Christ endures the shame of the cross in order to establish a new way of being in the world.

> For the message about the cross is foolishness to those who are perishing, but to us who are being saved it is the power

of God. . . . Consider your own call, brothers and sisters: not many of you were wise by human standards, not many were powerful, not many were of noble birth. But God chose what is foolish in the world to shame the wise; God chose what is weak in the world to shame the strong; God chose what is low and despised in the world, things that are not, to reduce to nothing things that are, so that no one might boast in the presence of God. He is the source of your life in Christ Jesus, who became for us wisdom from God, and righteousness and sanctification and redemption, in order that, as it is written, "Let the one who boasts, boast in the Lord." (1 Cor 1:18, 26-31)

In other words, the second Adam changes the relationship between God and humanity (cf. Gen 3) by embracing shame and not denying it or hiding from it. In identifying with human weakness and foolishness, God in Christ has redefined power and wisdom. We will see below in chapter five that in doing so, Christ has effectively dealt with our shame as well as our guilt.

The decisive work of Christ is further illustrated by what C. D. Schneider refers to as the "shamelessness of the New Testament."[20] What this means is that the other Greek word for shame (*aidōs*) appears only once. This was the positive understanding of shame that was linked to "awe for the sacred." Here shame is meant to be embraced and means the keeping of a proper distance from the holy things. Such an embrace of shame is lived out by rituals such as temple worship, ceremonial washing and other purity rites. But the New Testament systematically eliminates all these "shame-based" structures not by a more positive view of humanity (as if we were not sinners and can boldly approach God on that basis), but by the decisive acts of God in Jesus Christ where he has opened a way for us through the curtain (Heb 10:19-23), eliminated clean/unclean dietary scruples (Acts 10) and eventually eliminates temple worship all together (Rev 21:22). The heart of the relationship is changed dramatically in that we are invited to approach God as Jesus does: "Our Father—our Daddy." Those who once did not dare to utter the name of God are now allowed the most familiar and childlike forms of address.

When one turns to the psychological literature, Helen Block Lewis is often cited as a pioneer in making the important distinction between shame and guilt.[21] Building on her work, June Tangney and Ronda Dearing offer the following definitions based on their research. "Shame is an extremely painful and ugly feeling that has a negative impact on interpersonal behavior.... Guilt on the other hand may not be that bad after all."[22] Broadly speaking, those two definitions reveal that shame is far more debilitating to human functioning than is guilt. In their research, they discovered that because guilt is related to particular acts, the painful emotion of guilt can actually lead to specific actions that are attempts to salve the guilt. In contrast, shame does not move people toward constructive action.

One way to get at the difference is to imagine a common scenario. It is late at night and you are feeling hungry. Rummaging through the pantry, you spot a bag of chips. "I'll just have a couple," you reason to yourself, but because "no one can eat just one," before you know it, half the bag is gone. With morning comes the reckoning of the scale. Not liking what you read, the guilt response may go something like this: "Well, eating half a bag of chips late at night is not an intelligent thing to do. Tonight, if I get hungry, I'll have an apple." On the other hand, the shame response goes something along these lines: "What kind of a pig eats half a bag of chips? Is it any wonder I have so few friends and nobody really cares for me?" The same action yields two very different responses.

Another way to get at the difference between the two phenomena is to examine the role of the self. Shame is directly about the self. In terms of judgment, with shame it is the self that is found inadequate, whereas with guilt, particular actions are judged in negative terms. For that reason, guilt tends to be a far less painful experience. One can change or mend one's behaviors. But, how does one become a different self? If one cannot become someone else, the next best thing is to run and hide the shamed self that feels a universalized negative judgment.

This leads to some other interesting observations regarding shame. Unlike the feeling of guilt, which arises from a conflict between the self and external authorities (in Freudian terms, the ego and superego), shame involves an internal conflict within the self (the ego and ego ideal).

If guilt is the difference between knowing what we should do and not doing it, shame is the difference between knowing who we should be and not being that person. Guilt fears punishment; shame fears the loss of love.[23] Even as guilt occurs along a "good-bad" continuum, shame falls along a "strong-weak" continuum. In other words, the key concern for shame is not morality but adequacy. To feel guilty assumes a level of power to change one's behavior and thus oneself. Feelings of shame are normally accompanied by a deep sense of powerlessness. Thus the most natural response seems to be hiding, which is what any reasonable creature would do in the presence of a far stronger enemy.

Because of its internalized nature, shame has some pronounced physiological aspects: we blush when ashamed, we avert our eyes, cover our face, "sink into the ground" or even literally run away. In that shame is a much more strictly internal experience, it is also more intricately connected to feeling than is guilt. Most of us have encountered people who are guilty but do not feel guilty. (Just ask any prison warden!) On the other hand, one can feel guilty without actually being guilty. The objective reality of guilt does not always coincide with our experiences. But if a person feels ashamed, they are ashamed. For shame, there is no distance between the reality and the associated feelings.

Many developmental psychologists understand shame as the more primal of the two emotions (two-year-olds may experience shame, but probably not guilt). But it seems to be the case that the natural human inclination toward salvation is to change our behavior (try to be a better person and act differently). However, this behavior-based strategy does nothing to touch shame. One can know the good and still not have the power to do it. Thus no moral strategy is adequate to touch the foundation of shame. Even if we do the good 95 percent of the time, the problem of human inadequacy goes unresolved. That 5 percent still marks us with failure. Could this possibly be a part of what we mean in the Christian tradition by saying that we are unable to save ourselves? This has been illustrated principally in contemporary culture by twelve-step programs. All of these begin with the recognition and confession of one's powerlessness (weakness) to save oneself. In order to address adequately any addictive behavior, one must admit impotence. And to address such impotence is to own shame; there is no action one can take to improve one's status. Tangney and Dearing point out that the "fundamental difference between shame and guilt centers on the role of the self."[24] The self has some power to deal with guilt-related behaviors. That same self is paralyzed, however, when facing the depths of its inability to touch the core problem of shame.

It is for this reason that the person experiencing shame feels the desire to run and hide by either literally leaving the shaming environment or averting their eyes from the source of shame. Such tactics are, of course, never adequate because as the old saying goes, "No matter where you go, there you are!" It is impossible to run from shame because the shamed person takes the true source of shame (which is internal) with them. In this way, shame has a compounding quality: the sense of powerlessness causes the shamed person to feel even more ashamed. On the other hand, feelings of guilt presume much more optimistic scenarios. The guilty are able to perceive a different way of being (e.g., confession and repentance) that is within the realm of possibilities, although difficult. The shame-filled usually are unable to sense any way forward.

Shame responses are often out of proportion to the actual severity of an event. It is not uncommon for the shamed person to be the only one aware of the shame unless a reddened face gives the fact away. Persons experiencing shame feel acutely that they are being observed by others. It is not uncommon for the shamed to become more concerned about the opinions of others than their own self-evaluations. They tend to diminish and even negate their self-evaluations, judging them to be nontrustworthy.

Finally, shame appears to be peculiarly social, intimately linked to "face" and "losing face." To say that one is ashamed of oneself is to point to the connection of shame and one's identity. And in particular, shame is concerned with one's identity within a grouping of people. In fearing the perception of others, shame fears a loss of status within the group.

Because shame is such a debilitating experience, people tend to develop their own particular defending strategies against further shaming. Although these strategies are usually unconscious, there are several principle ones that people employ to avoid further humiliation. In his classic work, *Shame: The Power of Caring*, Gershen Kaufman lists six of these strategies.[25] First, *rage* is normally an extroverted response. Rage is an attempt to prevent further shaming and it can be a means by which a person shifts shame to another. The fear of further embarrassment is sensed, but it is anger that is expressed. These angry outbursts can be expressed as hostility toward particular people or can be internalized as bitterness at life in general.

The second defensive strategy is *contempt*. Contempt is usually manifest as a harsh judgmental attitude, fault finding or a condescending manner. With this defensive strategy, the shamed person responds by tearing down others. The person finds him- or herself as greatly lacking but treats others as even more inferior. So fearing the judgment of others, he or she judges others as inadequate.

Third is the *striving for power*. Recall again that shame causes a person to feel weak, inadequate and powerless. A common compensatory strategy is the attempt to gain maximum control of all situations. In this scenario, the shamed person feels that the more control they have, the less potential there is for further shame. The need to "always be on top" becomes the primary way to see that others are shamed rather than oneself.

The fourth strategy is *striving for perfection*. A shamed person feels defective. This strategy is often manifested because a person has never learned "how much is good enough." Because such people cope with a harsh internal standard they desire to measure their value by means of exterior comparisons. This is frequently manifested by an extremely competitive spirit; such people feel devastated unless they win, no matter how trivial the contest may be. Even small loses are experienced as significant for fear that they betray the less-than-optimum truth of their lives.

The next way in which some people deal with potential shame is the *transference of blame*. Perceived through a lens of shame, even small problems are understood to be unfixable. So when the "blame game" becomes truly toxic, repairing a difficult situation is no longer considered. Instead, the primary goal is to assign blame: "Whose fault is this?" Eventually, the pattern leads to a scapegoating mentality where particular people or even groups of people become identified as the source of the problem. Paradoxically, however, blame shifting only increases one's shame, since one assumes that other parties are always responsible for life's difficulties. Such thinking only reinforces one's perceptions of personal weakness and therefore compounds a sense of shame. In a similar manner, one can too quickly accept blame. Children who are consistently blamed for family problems can adapt the coping strategy of self-blame in order to preempt harsher parental blaming.

Finally, some shame-filled people may adopt a strategy of *internal withdrawal*. More likely practiced by introverts, internal withdrawal employs a retreat into a fantasy alternative reality wherein the shamed person imagines having a greatness that goes unrecognized by others. For those who practice such a strategy, it becomes increasingly tempting to spend more and more time within that alternative reality. One must wonder how some contemporary technology increases the ease of using such a coping mechanism. Some social media aids the creation of a false (better?) self. "I must be a likeable person because I have thousands of friends!" At one level, however, that person still knows who he or she really is and therefore still fears exposure.

Before moving on, it is important to note that all people experiencing shaming events may employ the above-mentioned strategies rather than face the pain of embarrassment. The deeper problems occur when the strategies become habitual and cause the person to fail to deal with the shaming experiences in helpful ways. In a parallel manner it is easy to see that particular shame-defense strategies may be identified with particular sins that Michael Mangis refers to as "signature sins."[26] Perhaps the seven deadly sins (pride, envy, wrath, etc.) are only another way to describe the particular and inadequate ways in which people deal with the core problem of shame. In the next chapter, we will examine in detail the relationship between original sin and shame.

THE OVEREMPHASIS ON GUILT IN WESTERN THEOLOGY

We have been discussing the problem of understanding and appropriating forgiveness in the contemporary context. Up to this point, we have been critical of our therapeutic context and its tendency to turn forgiveness and reconciliation into a human project. At the same time, we have discovered that there are important insights to be discovered by way of the social sciences. The distinction between guilt and shame helps us take up a second and equally important part of our critique: traditional atonement theories. Before addressing the critique, however, it will be necessary to describe those theories.

There can be no doubt that central to the Christian faith is the belief that Jesus Christ came into the world in order to forgive our sin and to restore us to fellowship with the God who created us. But once that basic affirmation is made, a number of questions arise. Most important is the question of *how*. How did

Jesus accomplish our forgiveness and reconciliation? That question has been answered in various ways throughout Christian history and all of the "classic" answers have been grounded in the witness of Scripture.

It should not surprise us that the solution to the central problem of humanity is not easy to describe. The earliest attempts by Christian thinkers to explain how Jesus accomplishes his mighty acts are no less simple. Irenaeus of Lyons (130–202) illustrates the complexity of speaking of Christ's work even as he adopts a general understanding of recapitulation. That means that the man Jesus does all that is necessary to reverse the human problem and to restore us to our original fellowship with God. In describing this recapitulation, Irenaeus employs a number of accounts of what is accomplished in Christ's work: "In sum, we find in Irenaeus a concept or hermeneutic of recapitulation, enabling him to offer a unified reading of the Old and New Testaments in light of the work of Christ. This reading is complex and varied, pulling together a whole range of explanations of Christ's death and resurrection."[27] In other words, the earliest attempt to offer a model of Jesus' atoning work made no attempt to distill the various biblical accounts into any simple theory.

It is only in the second millennium of Christian thinking that "one-dimensional" ideas about Christ's work emerged.[28] On the one hand, because our faith is evangelical at its core, that is, it is meant to be shared with others, we should not be surprised that the Christian theological tradition naturally moved to *shorthand* ways of describing what Jesus accomplishes on our behalf. Telling the story to others will naturally lead to simplified versions of the story. At the same time, however, it is important to keep in mind that such one-dimensional ideas simultaneously obscure the truth as well as illuminate it. In other words, they tend to oversimplify the reality of what Christ accomplishes on our behalf.[29]

THREE PRIMARY MODELS

One of the earliest models is referred to by different names: a ransom theory, the "fish hook" theory or Christus Victor.[30] What all three have in common is that the atonement is aimed primarily at the forces of evil, which may be described in various ways: Satan, the devil, powers or principalities. Whatever language is employed for those forces, they have one thing in common: they hold sway over sinful humanity. The atonement is conceived of as the way in which the power of those forces is broken so that humanity is set free from its prison and empowered to love God and neighbor with a new freedom. Jesus becomes the hostage taken in our place and the hook by which the devil is caught. The devil's power over humanity is broken.[31]

The second major Western theory is the moral example.[32] Usually associated with Peter Abelard (1079–1142), this theory is often the most modern sounding to contemporary ears. To behold Jesus on the cross works a change within us. In looking at Jesus hanging there, we see the "perfect manifestation in human form of God's self-sacrificial, condescending love, a helpful example for our imitation or morally powerful influence, spurring us to a similar love."[33] As we look to Jesus, we should be so filled of appreciation for what God has done that we change our wicked ways and begin to lead a new life. The imitation of Christ becomes important here. We too, having caught this vision of sacrificial love, ought to be empowered to live likewise. To ask, what would Jesus do? in any given situation reflects this new way of living.

The most influential model in Western theological reflection is the penal substitution theory. Our sin is an affront to God's justice and cannot abide in the presence of his holiness. But at the same time, God still loves us and so takes on human flesh in order to pay the penalty for sin that we cannot repay. In his dying, Jesus has substituted his life for ours and therefore a way is cleared for us to repent and believe in him, being taken up in this profound act of grace. This model came to preeminence in the West with Anselm of Canterbury (1033–1109) and his *Cur Deus Homo*, "Why did God become human?" Despite its medieval lineage, the theory came to a special prominence in the later nineteenth and early twentieth centuries, so that for many (and particularly evangelical Protestants) it became the only true explanation for Jesus' work on the cross.[34] For many contemporary Christians, this model remains the only way to make sense of how God answers the problem of human sin.

Each of the three atonement models has a basis in Scripture. Each one has been proposed and developed by intelligent and faithful Christians. Taken together, they do offer an expansive understanding of the central belief of Christianity. At the same time, however, each one in the Western church has led to an obscuring of God's activity rather than to its illumination. We now turn to the reason for that.

THE LATIN HERESY

At the conclusion of the last chapter we made reference to the way in which therapy's focus on better functioning causes it to be one more example of what T. F. Torrance has described as the "Latin heresy."[35] This may seem to be somewhat obscure, so some explanation is necessary. The Latin heresy refers to the peculiarly Western church's understanding that when the Son of God, the second person of the Trinity, took on human nature, it was a neutral nature. That is, his nature did not participate in human sin like our own does.[36] In spite of the relative obscurity of this doctrine, the problems that it causes should not be underestimated. Most importantly, if Jesus assumed an unbroken human nature, he always remains at a certain distance from us. Since Irenaeus, the church had placed an emphasis on the necessity of Jesus assuming all of humanity that was in need of healing. Thus, Irenaeus emphasized the importance of Christ *recapitulating* all that we are. It is the very act of that recapitulation that brings us reconciliation and forgiveness. But now, with this "new" teaching, God's act of forgiveness becomes understood as a transaction that remains external from us. It is something that only has the power to save us once we act on it. The healing of our alienation becomes contingent on our reception of this external work. The atonement, understood in this way, is an offer from God to us demanding some form of response. Those who respond are saved.

Furthermore, if the Son of God does not assume our broken humanity, he does not really address our original or our basic identification with sin. The focus of the atonement will always be on guilt because Jesus has dealt with the guilt of our individual sins, but not the basic problem of our broken identity. It is for precisely this reason that the Western church has been focused on guilt and has essentially ignored the greater problem unleashed by human sin: our shame. If Jesus does not really share our identity, if he has not assumed our essential brokenness, how can our shame be touched? In this way, we see the second culprit responsible for the problem of forgiveness— much of Western theology!

So, what if much of Western theology has misunderstood the nature of the atonement? What if the atonement and the incarnation are not two separate acts, but one and the same? What if in Christ's assuming our humanity in all of its sinful failure, God in Christ has not been polluted by us but instead has transformed our very status? With the incarnation, we have far more than a model of behavior; instead, we have a new identity in Christ. This does not mean that our human response is of no consequence. But it can never be forgotten that such response is only possible because of the profound transformation accomplished by the Son of God's incarnation. God has entered human history and therefore humanity is different; a new Adam is present in Jesus Christ. Both theology and therapy's focus on human behavior always tends to hide or diminish the full truth of what God has done, not just for us, but within us. The saving activity of the triune God has not only addressed the guilt of our behavior but has also transformed our shame with a new identity. From this vantage point, one may begin to read with new eyes the Scriptures, which are authoritatively descriptive of both our sin and our redemption. In particular, we now turn to the Genesis stories of the origin of sin in order to discover the way in which shame has been addressed all along.

FOUR

Opened Eyes and Downturned Faces

Essential to the task of receiving and offering forgiveness is to gain a better understanding of the guilt and shame distinction as we have taken it up in the last chapter. Seeing the difference between the two, we may now begin to understand sin in a new way. In general terms, we may reemploy the classic Christian distinction between original sin and our individual sins. That is, we are all sinners in two distinct ways. First, in various and sundry manner, we do things that are wrong and we also fail to do the things that are right. Such failures make us objectively guilty and as a result much of the time our feelings correspond so that we feel subjectively guilty. But this penchant for sinning reveals a deeper problem. Our lack of neutrality, our curvature back on ourselves, our inability to cease from sinning displays our prior problem: we are born broken. All of us do evil and fail to do good. And this is our shame.

Humanity, of course, occupies a special place in the creation. All of the created order is pronounced *good* again and again (see Gen 1:4, 10, 12, 18, 21, 25) but after the creation of humanity, male and female, Genesis 1 culminates with the pronouncement that all things are *very good* (Gen 1:31). Humanity is given a particular status—a particular part of the created order is given a place of authority within that created order.

Genesis 2 further reveals that particular status. The Creator God desires fellowship with humanity and is especially concerned that humanity not be alone (Gen 2:18-20). So we have a reiteration of our creation, culminating again with the good words that the human being is not alone, a companion has been given and the two are naked and not ashamed (Gen 2:25). And it is exactly at this point that the problem begins.

In light of the guilt and shame distinctions, when one examines again the biblical story of the entry of sin into human experience, something quite remarkable begins to happen. One of the most well-known stories subtly changes, which should help us better understand how we experience the brokenness of sin. Beginning with Genesis 3:1 ("Now the serpent was more crafty than any other wild animal that the LORD God had made. He said to the woman, 'Did God say, "You shall not eat from any tree in the garden"?'"), we observe that the serpent's initial question is the attempt to raise some doubt, to create some distance between the Creator and the pinnacle of the creation, humanity. Dietrich Bonhoeffer refers to this as "the first pious question in the world."[1] By this he means that the temptation is a subtle one. Perhaps the serpent is only looking to increase its own knowledge of God. But here is exactly where the problem begins: the serpent has proposed an abstract God, a God who is separate from his direct presence and word to humanity. And Eve falls for it. In essence she joins the serpent in its philosophical (dare we say, theological) discussion by also positing a God beyond the one that she knows. This occurs when she adds to the prohibition: "Nor shall you touch it" (Gen 3:3). Some scholars over the years have thought that it is exactly here where the fall occurs. For it is in this place that the relationship with the one true God is breached.

The initial break in our relationship with God is constituted by a lack of faith that God's Word is trustworthy. Up until this point, the Word of God has always been characterized by its goodness. It has continuously celebrated the goodness of the creation and especially humanity's place in it. Up until this point, God has only shown loving compassion and joy in all aspects of the created order. But, by adding to the prohibition, we see that the primordial temptation is to trade our relationship with God for a principle by which we may have direct access to the knowledge of good and evil. Such a principle provides an existential and rhetorical place for us that is over and against God, that ultimately allows us to argue directly against God's Word. "Did God really say that? That doesn't sound very loving and generous; that can't be what he meant." At this point, the damage is done; we no longer believe that we can take God at his word. A shadow has fallen and there is distance and mistrust in the relationship. From this point forward, we will (and believe that we must) interpret according to our own understanding, thinking it to be a more accurate representation of the truth. Our dependence on our relationship with God has been supplemented by our own independent judgment and by doing so, the relationship has been superseded.

The way in which the breach in relationship is experienced is contained in the serpent's second statement of what will really happen: their "eyes will open" and they will be "like God" (*sicut Deus* in the Latin).[2]

NAKED AND ASHAMED

It is to shame that we must now return, for that is the second part of the serpent's statement: their "eyes are opened." And what does the first couple see? They are naked. Citing Genesis 2:25 ("And the man and his wife were both naked, and were not ashamed") Bonhoeffer states,

> The shame of human beings is an unwilling pointer to revelation, to the limit, to the other, to God. For that reason the persistence of shame in the fallen world constitutes the only—even though an extremely contradictory—possibility of a sign pointing to original nakedness and the sanctity of this nakedness. This is not because shame in itself is something good—that is the moralistic, puritanical, and totally unbiblical interpretation—but because it is compelled to give unwilling witness to the fallen state of the ashamed.[3]

The opening of the first couple's eyes, the first realization of "nakedness" implies several consequential results. First, we see that shame is the price of the loss of relationship between Creator and creature. Our opened eyes are the eyes that must now arbitrate all reality through our own meager resources. Bowed beneath the weight of judging good from evil, our faces are cast downward and we are forced to see ourselves naked. But this is not the nakedness of innocence, of life lived in unity with God and neighbor. This is the nakedness of a counterreality—a life wrenched from relationship. As the judges of good and evil, we must now also maintain a dim awareness of our finitude even in our attempts at divinity (*sicut Deus*). Our eyes are opened and we realize that we do not have the strength to fulfill the task of determining what is good and what is evil. The need for covering ourselves is the implicit acknowledgement that we are not who we claim to be: independent, limitless and self-creating. The covering of ourselves reveals shame that is the acknowledgement that we abide within the sight of the other and that we fear their judgment of us. We fear that they will come to realize who we really are: not all-powerful, but broken and weak.

Recall again that the etymology of the word *shame* is to cover or to hide. The original break in fellowship with God ushered in a new sense of self-awareness. Human beings made in the image of the triune God are personal at their very core. What this implies, in part, is that like the three persons of the Trinity, we are essentially subjects and are never meant to be treated as objects. The divine interrelations among the Father, Son and Holy Spirit interpenetrate rather than objectify. What that means is that the three persons remain united while simultaneously unique. Traditional theology has termed this "perichoretic coactivity." It is the traditional (and perhaps rather obscure) way to state that the perfect love that exists among the three divine persons never objectifies the other; it never overwhelms or minimizes the complete subjectivity of the other.

Sin changes all that for human beings. Shame objectifies, turning the self into an object. In the process the key human self-potential is lost by basing one's identity in the perception of the other. Shame forces us to think of ourselves principally from the perspective of another. "What does the other think?" becomes more important than "What do I think?" Simultaneously, fearing judgment, shame objectifies the other. They can never be treated as subject. They become the object of our fears. Cut off from the loving interpenetrating relating of the God revealed in Scripture, we *sicut Deus* humans lack the power to live as we desire.

At the same time, however, shame can still be understood in a positive light. As the image bearers (*imago Dei*) of the triune God, we were created in and can only thrive through relationship. Even though it may be difficult to admit, we crave and rightly need the positive acknowledgement of the other. It is then possible to conclude that shame is the consequential response of *imago Dei* humanity trying to live as *sicut Deus* humanity. We have been created in such a way that all of our attempts at an independent individualism will leave us feeling weak and alienated. Shame's ambiguity is known in our inconsistent and seemingly contradictory feelings. Karl Barth says it well:

> It is because they are held by God and cannot escape that they see that they are fleeing from Him; and it is because they are not let go and finally abandoned that they see that they are held. Known sin is always forgiven sin, known in the light of forgiveness and the triumphant grace of God. . . . Unforgiven sin, or sin not yet known to be forgiven, is always unrecognized sin.[4]

As negative as the experience of shame is, it still can be an indication that there is something better than that for which we would settle.

Positively speaking, shame is the consequence of a life that is lived out of joint. The Christian who experiences shame may understand the unpleasant feeling as the natural response of those who really belong to God, trying to live independently of that God. The answer to shame is not running but allowing oneself to be embraced. Shame reminds us that we really are not who we would claim to be. Thus, shame is a universal experience in a way that guilt is not. Guilt is always specific to particular actions or failures to act. Guilt is only secondarily universal insofar as people who are ashamed respond to the other in inappropriate ways. Fearing negative judgment, we may lash out in anger or emotionally withdraw from the other. Several of these impotent attempts to avoid shame are on full display by our primordial parents.[5]

Returning to Genesis 3, something odd has happened in the first couple's experience of their disobedience. As we have seen, guilt is the associated experience of doing something wrong, like breaking a commandment. Our parents break a known law of God for which they should experience the associated feelings of guilt. But something different happens. Their hiding is not the classic response to guilt, but to shame. They don't try to hide their sin (we have no record of an attempt to tie the fruit back on the tree!); they try to hide themselves. In its etymology, shame literally refers to "covering." For a microsecond they "were like God" (*sicut Deus*) but reality reasserts itself and the greatest terror of all comes upon them and all of us who follow: reality no longer appears the same. The primordial parents now perceive everything differently. Perception is no longer centered in terms of God, their Creator and loving friend, but now all things are perceived in terms of themselves and those selves are desperately broken. A gap has emerged between the self and the *imago Dei* that continues to remain central to human identity. But it is no longer the glory of humanity to bear God's image; now it is perceived as a terrible burden and hindrance to human freedom.

Adam and Eve first try to flee from their own eyes, from the eyes of the other and from God. What must have once been the highlight of existence, when God joined them in fellowship, has now become horrible. God is no longer perceived as the intimate friend, but now as an alien and all-powerful judge of the new self-understanding. Once confronted, the first couple employ the defending strategy of transferring blame (Gen 3:11-13). Eve shifts blame to the serpent but Adam shows the ripening of shame in that he simultaneously blames Eve and God ("The woman whom you gave to be with me")! Adam shows that shame has not only broken his relationship with God but now with his wife. They are no longer coregents under the Creator, but competitors. Humanity no longer naturally turns to the neighbor in order to participate fully in God's glory. Instead, the neighbor is shunned. He or she is no longer perceived as helpmate or completion of the self, but as other—as stranger and potential rival. Time will allow other strategies to manifest themselves (as we will see below) but hiding and blame shifting seem to be the most primordial for humanity according to Genesis 3.

THE ORIGINS OF CONSCIENCE

One could argue that the human conscience actually emerges with our fall, with our break with fellowship with God.[6] Our shame forces us to hide from God and the primary place in which we hide is our conscience. Our conscience, rather than being an objective voice of judgment, is biased. It is not an objective voice of reality. Conscience reminds us that feelings of shame are not simply those times in which we feel embarrassed, humiliated or inadequate. Instead, shame is the natural state of humanity. Even in apparent times of human strength and triumph, we are shame-filled. Shame is our experience of being the solitary arbiter of what is good and what is evil. In our attempts to function as the Creator rather than as a part of the Creation, we ultimately fail, feeling weak and inadequate. The primary manifestations of our shame are our attempts to be the judges of God, our neighbors and ourselves.

John Watson has observed that shame turns God from our healer into our accuser.[7] It is in this way that shame causes us to fear rather than to trust God.

We noted the inadequacy of conscience in the last chapter. Perhaps a better way to understand the conscience is to see it as the chief protector of the *sicut Deus* self. Our conscience is the way that we judge ourselves and others in order to preserve our inadequate self-understanding. From time to time, the conscience does stumble upon a realistic judgment, but it may never be trusted to be a faithful arbiter of the truth of our lives or the lives of others. Furthermore, our conscience not only becomes the means by which we accuse ourselves and our neighbors; we also use it against God. Adam and Eve's arguing with God show us an age-old pattern of avoiding the truth of our lives. With this new standard of judgment, we can no longer recognize the reality of who God is and who we are in relationship to him.[8]

Without knowing it, in our self-absorbed, shame-filled categories we have become disabled from hearing the grace of God's call. God speaks in love and seeks fellowship. We hear condemnation and anger. Make no mistake, the question, "Where are you?" (Gen 3:9) is not seeking Adam and Eve's location. God's question is a judgment and at the same time, an attempt to help the lost realize that they are lost. Adam's response reveals one of the central issues that are confronted when dealing with human brokenness: How do we help people hear, "Where are you?" as coming from the God who loves them? How do we help people realize that the question is being asked by the Judge who has accepted judgment in our place? Even in the primordial story of the first offense, we behold God, the jilted lover who goes seeking and reaching out to the ones who have betrayed his love.

As we focus on God's question, "Adam, where are you?" we come to realize that God will not allow us to remain alone in our sin. He calls to us and demands that we reveal ourselves.[9] It is ultimately impossible for *imago Dei* humankind to remain alone. We were not created for hiding. Humankind will be sought out; they will be discovered and held within the sight of the One whose image they bear. We are very much like Adam and Eve who refuse to reveal themselves, to be seen again. In our unwillingness to be seen, we can never adequately know and thus be our true selves.

Contemporary Western culture places great emphasis on that same admonition: "Be your true self!" But what if we don't really know who we are? What if our shame and guilt have blinded us to seeing our true selves? *Sicut Deus* humans still bear *imago Dei*, but we function as if that is not the case. Many of us spend much of our lives moving from one self to the next. We desperately want to be our true selves but we have forgotten who those selves are. We will see in the final chapter that because we are *imago Dei* creatures and only falsely *sicut Deus* creatures we can never know ourselves absent from our relationships. Insofar as shame debilitates relationships, it also makes it impossible for us to know our true selves and thus to be ourselves. It is not just God from whom we hide; we hide from each other as well. In our fear, we may even begin to hate those from whom we hide.

Genesis 3 ends with the banishment of Adam and Eve from paradise. By taking the fruit of the tree of the knowledge of good and evil, humanity has ipso facto cut itself off from the tree of life. This is usually seen as a part of God's judgment on sin, which it is. But what if it is also part of God's gracious intervention in the sinful humiliation of humanity? There is an old Russian proverb that says, "Shame is worse than death." Perhaps the entrance of death at the conclusion of the story is the triune God's loving limiting of our shame. Could there be a worse hell than to live with an unending sense of shame? What if it is not wrath that ushers death into the goodness of creation, but love? Adam and Eve now walk the road of death, the way of *sicut Deus* humanity. Unable to abide in God's presence they must find a place out of view. With that, we turn to the Bible's next story, the next chapter in the story of shame.

IN THE KINGDOM OF SHAME

Shame-based reality creates the war of all against all. No one is perceived in strictly neutral terms. All are potentially judges of the inadequate self, all are potentially enemies who may come to unmask the truth of our lives. Because of its suspicious nature, this new shame reality is destructive of all relationships, even (and perhaps especially) the closest ones. This is well illustrated in Genesis 4:1-16, the story of Cain and Abel. Genesis 4 illustrates how shame makes it difficult to abide lovingly in the presence of others. The story of the first brothers is also the primordial story of the first murder. Rivalry is the natural conclusion of shame-filled lives. This is the origin of the "zero-sum game." There is a scarcity of love and honor in this new way of thinking and in the very perception of the world. If God favors one, it must naturally mean that he does not love the other. Ultimately Cain cannot bear to be with Abel once he is perceived as the rival and especially as the one whose sacrifice has been accepted. Shame shuns community because the presence of others is perceived as a threat. Shamed eyes cannot meet the eyes of others. All others are potential enemies to the fragile ego that attempts to live *sicut Deus*.[10]

The horrible rules of conduct in the kingdom of shame offer no other possibility for us because we are only pretenders to the title of *sicut Deus*. It is not who we really are and we cannot storm the gates of paradise. We cannot really give or sustain life on our own. All of our life-creating and life-perpetuating work only occurs on the way of death. The human way of death over life is vividly displayed by Cain. The first fratricide reveals that no relationships are safe in the kingdom of shame.

GOD'S QUESTIONS TO THOSE WHO WOULD HIDE

In Genesis 3 and 4 we see that God's reconciling work to restore fellowship with sinful humanity is marked by several questions. They may be distinguished as questions to the guilty and questions to the ashamed. God approaches shame first in Genesis 3:9 as the question goes to Adam and Eve, "Where are you?" That is the question of identity. God is seeking the whole persons; he is not yet inquiring about their behavior. God is seeking to first locate us as the persons whom he has created. That question is followed by the inquiry to the guilty: "What have you done?" (Gen 3:11). This is the behavior-specific question. What have you done that has prompted your disappearance? What law have you broken that forces you to run and hide from your Lord and friend?

We see this same sequence of questions in Genesis 4:9. God asks Cain, "Where is your brother?" Again, this is the question of identity. By asking Cain about Abel's location, God is forcing Cain to recall that he is in relationship with his brother. In giving his reply, Cain of course attempts to establish a shame-based identity that is not grounded in relationship. To ask, "Am I my brother's keeper?" is our attempt to live life alone. It is our effort to construct an independent self who lives as if relationships are unnecessary or only tangential to the self. The universal nature of shame reminds us that whether we ask Cain's question or not, we are prone to live as if we are self-adequate.

Once again, the follow-up question in Genesis 4:10, "What have you done?" addresses the issue of guilt. What the two chapters and four questions show is the necessity that shame must be dealt with prior to guilt. Only after the shamed are called out can they face the truth of their actions. We will further explore the sequence of these two questions in chapters five and six.

In looking at several of the details of Genesis 4, we may observe that in Genesis 4:5-7, Cain's offering is rejected. In spite of many attempts to advance a reason for the rejection (Cain's attitude, a lack of quality in what is sacrificed, etc.) the text refuses to offer a reason for the lack of acceptance. What the text does assert is that Cain himself is *not* rejected. God does not condemn Cain, only his action. And yet again, we see the shame response. Cain becomes angry and his countenance falls. With face pointed down we see the classic shame response of looking away from others that is accompanied by a collapse inward upon the self. Furthermore, recalling Kaufman's strategies for defending against further shame,[11] Cain becomes enraged, blaming his brother Abel.

Yet, even here, God intervenes, offering a response to Cain's shame: "The LORD said to Cain, 'Why are you angry, and why has your countenance fallen? If you do well, will you not be accepted? And if you do not do well, sin is lurking at the door; its desire is for you, but you must master it'" (Gen 4:6-7). There is a certain ambiguity in the original Hebrew of these verses, but Gerhard von Rad makes an important observation: "Unfortunately, the statement is in part really obscure. . . . V. 7a can in our opinion be understood neither in the sense of forgiveness nor of the presentation or acceptance of the sacrifice; rather, one must relate it to *panim*, 'face' (in contrast to the *napal*, 'fall,' in verse 6b): 'If you do well, there is lifting up,' i.e., you can freely lift up your face."[12]

God is not only warning Cain, he is also reminding him that he can be restored to relationship with God and the brother whom he now hates. "Lift up your face! Look away from yourself and turn again to the essence of who you really are: *imago Dei*, one who has been created for relationship." In addressing Cain here, God is creating space between Cain, himself and his actions. Cain has apparently failed in some way in the offered sacrifice. But God's unwillingness to accept the sacrifice does not mean that God is unwilling to accept Cain. Tragically, Cain will not accept God's overture and succumbs to his rage.

And so the first murder occurs in the Scriptures and the aftermath is terrible. Cain is sentenced to wander insofar as the cursed and now contaminated land will no longer cooperate with the murderer. Cain objects to the harshness of the consequences of his sin, and God has mercy. The famous "mark" is placed upon him. It can be argued that the mark has a double meaning. It is, of course, a sign of shame. Cain has done something terrible and his very identity is changed as a result. Yet, at the same time, the mark is a sign of protection. In spite of his sin, Cain remains in relationship to the God who created him and continues to love him. Walter Brueggemann observes that

> God does not let go of the unreconciled one. The God who calls the worlds into being does not stop calling, even this chaotic brother. He marks him with a mark signifying both shame and security. The mystery of God is that God's

protection extends now to the land of Nod (v. 16) to the place thought beyond protection, the place that seemed beyond humanness.[13]

Even wrathful, wandering Cain cannot fully escape the God who loves him and cares for him. Cain's mark, which represents both "shame and security," is borne by all who suffer the shaming effects of sin. All who experience shame continue to bear God's image as sinners, which shames but may also remind one that God continues to recognize, seek and offer reconciliation and restoration. We will see below the way in which this is accomplished.

In closing, Bonhoeffer succinctly states the problem of sin and its resulting shame.

> Instead of seeing God man sees himself. . . . Man perceives himself in his disunion with God and with men. He perceives that he is naked. Lacking the protection, the covering, which God and his fellow-man afforded him, he finds himself laid bare. Hence there arises shame. Shame is man's ineffaceable recollection of his estrangement from the origin; it is grief for this estrangement, and the powerless longing to return to unity with the origin.[14]

This definition of shame is an insightful one and summarizes well what we have examined in this chapter. It shows the deep connection between present experience and human origins. It points us backward to our true identity, which is found to be painful due to our alienation from it. Shame, we discover, is inescapable on our part because of who we really are: image bearers of God. What was our crowning glory is now the horrible burden of a general sense of failure: failure to achieve, failure to relate to God and to neighbor in noncompetitive ways. God is now threat; neighbor is now potentially dangerous because of our sense of exposure. The sense of exposure is what we feel in trying to master reality, in seeking to perceive reality in terms of our own understanding of good and evil. Again, all this is tragic in that shame need no longer be the basis for our relationship to God. We, like Adam and Eve, no longer need hide. We are again privileged to walk with God in the cool of the day. This new potential is due to the intervening and reconciling work of the triune God, to which we now turn.

FIVE

THE SHAME OF THE CROSS

The classic atonement model of penal substitution understands that the Son in his humanity pays a price that no other human can pay. All individual humans who trust Jesus' atoning work find their individual guilt assuaged. And so as we become aware of our sin, repent and turn to Christ, we are judged "not guilty." God is satisfied and a new relationship may begin. As long as guilt is humanity's primary problem, penal substitution provides a helpful way to make sense of the atonement. I am not attempting to argue against the reality of human guilt. I am in complete agreement with Paul when he reminds the Christians in Rome and us that "all have sinned and fall short of the glory of God" (Rom 3:23). But what happens when guilt is no longer understood to be the primary human predicament? What happens when another problem inhibits us from owning our guilt, from being able to repent and trust Christ, who has paid the price for us?

Furthermore, what happens when the church continues to give answers to questions that the world is no longer asking? Many would agree that in the West, we are now in a post-Christendom culture. By that, I mean that Christianity can no longer be assumed to be central to the lives of most people. Both church membership and church attendance are down. Most clergy no longer occupy places of prestige in the larger community. Increasingly, they are not sought out for advice. In many places, the church is not noticed, let alone authoritative. Does this mean that the church no longer has a role to play in Western culture? I would argue that is not the case. At the same time, that does not mean that we may keep up a "business as usual" approach. It is important that the church listen first so that it may effectively tell again the "old, old story." It is important that we make sure that the central teaching of our faith, the work of Jesus Christ, be offered is such a way that it may be heard. In part, this will mean a new emphasis on Christ's triumph over shame.

LEARNING FROM THE HOLOCAUST:
THE RETURN OF SHAME

Ruth Leys offers considerable insight into the replacement of guilt by shame in the postwar West.[1] Her primary concern focuses on the loss of responsibility that is implied by the marginalization of guilt. Guilt's focus on actions taken allows for an assessment of responsibility. Her particular area of examination is the minimization of "survivor guilt" in the diagnosis of post-traumatic stress syndrome. Leys cites an almost "missionary zeal" in the replacement of shame with guilt for understanding properly the traumatic state.[2] Her work is an attempt to examine the consequences of such a substitution.

Citing the work of Giorgio Agamben,[3] Leys states that "the concentration camps were nothing less than an 'absolute situation' that revealed shame to be 'truly something like the hidden structure of all subjectivity and consciousness.'"[4] This is a remarkable statement that parallels Bonhoeffer's understanding of conscience covered in the last chapter. Shame is not something that only a few experience at particularly difficult times. Instead, "absolute situations" reveal the true nature of the human dilemma. The locus of the human problem is not only in one's intentionality or actions, but in one's identity. What we have done does not explain all our problems. What has been done to us does not account for all our difficulties. The problem is not in our "stars" but in "ourselves."[5]

One of the most literate and heartbreaking examples of the movement from guilt to shame is found in the work of Holocaust survivor Primo Levi.[6] In *The Drowned and the Saved*,[7] Levi writes that both the Russian soldiers who liberated Auschwitz and the surviving inmates felt great shame. One should note here that Levi is not working with guilt and shame as separate categories and so he conflates them. Levi observes, "That many (including me) experienced 'shame,' that is, a feeling of guilt during the imprisonment and afterward, is an ascertained fact confirmed by numerous testimonies."[8]

He illustrates well the connection between shame and weakness. "Anyone who had the ability and will to act in this way, to oppose in this or other ways the machine of the Lager, was beyond the reach of 'shame'—or at least the shame of which I am speaking, because perhaps he experiences something else."[9] The outward turn to another dismantles the self-collapse of shame. At the same time, such acts, even while demonstrating a degree of strength, were often inherently selfish. One survived by placing one's own needs before anything else. Given the terrible nature of the concentration camps, such actions are completely rational and understandable.

And so often, a person survived through the failures of "human solidarity."[10] Even during the daily horrors of the concentration camp one could experience guilt after the failure to share with or help a fellow inmate in one way or another. At the end of the day, some were still able to reason that things might have been done differently. But once the camps were liberated, the guilt of the failure to act transformed into the shame of survival. The mere state of having survived the Nazi Holocaust changed everything. Something horrible about humanity had been revealed and everyone was the worse for it.[11] "It is no more than a supposition, indeed the shadow of a suspicion: that each man is his brother's Cain, that each one of us (but this time I say 'us' in a much vaster, indeed, universal sense) has usurped his neighbor's place and lived in his stead."[12]

"Each man is his brother's Cain. . . ." One survived at the expense of others. A new identity was born: survivor. But to survive meant the pressing anguish of still beholding in the mind's eye the faces of the better people who died in one's place. Levi identifies with Cain who lives but must wander alone, forever seeing his brother's face in his (shame-filled) imagination. But shame comes to more than those who directly experience the horrors of the Holocaust.

> And there is another, vaster shame, the shame of the world.
> . . . And yet there are those who, faced by the crime of others
> or their own, turn their backs so as not to see it and not feel
> touched by it. This is what the majority of Germans did
> during the twelve Hitlerian years, deluding themselves that
> not seeing was a way of not knowing, and that not knowing
> relieved them of their share of complicity or connivance.[13]

The most universal shame is the unwillingness or inability to look upon the suffering of the other. The world turns away. Unimaginable events such as the Holocaust illustrate the human potential for the refusal and inability to see the other as brother or sister. Through looking away, the self may be preserved; but it is a self that deems itself weak and inadequate, unable to cope with such a shame-filled identity.

A SHAME-CENTERED ATONEMENT MODEL

How can the church address such horrors if it is only able to speak the language of guilt? What happens when a culture is informed more by the shame of a selfish identity than it is by particular wrongful acts? Does Christ still have the power to address the darkness of the human situation?

For our purposes, the work of Leys and Levi help us to see that an atonement model directed toward shame is important for missional reasons. C. Norman Kraus and Mark Baker have both written eloquently regarding the importance of a shame-centered idea of atonement.[14] Kraus's work in particular is grounded in his missionary experience. He realized during his ministry in Japan that a shame-based culture such as Japan's often failed to appropriate a presentation of the gospel that focused on the alleviation of guilt.[15] Leys and Levi help us see further that a shame-based atonement model would be important for the contemporary West. Such a model need not deny the traditional forensic categories that focus on human guilt; that is, it was my sin that took Jesus to the cross. He paid the penalty that was my responsibility to pay, but I was unable to do so. A shame-based model need not deny accountability. Instead, it expands and adds greater depth to the traditional substitutionary categories.

The good news, as we have seen, is that unlike many modern Christians, the Bible addresses shame as well as guilt. And so we turn now to the way in which the triune God explicitly deals with human shame. In order to understand this, we must recall that shame strikes at the heart of human relationships. The down-turned face signals a collapse upon the self. Shame isolates the shamed one from others. Shame is a social phenomenon, grounded in the fear that the eyes of the other will not look upon the shamed one with admiration. Even as the shamed one is left alone contemplating the broken and weak self, others tend to look away because of shame's contagious nature. We fear the shame of the other because it reminds us of our own shame. And so it goes. The one who needs reassurance, the one who needs the face that will not turn aside, gets the opposite. We look away fearing contagion; we look away fearing that we too might be discovered for who we really are.

It is therefore necessary that because of shame's social con-struction we must approach the atonement in social terms. It is exactly at this point that many atonement theories go wrong. All too often the atonement is understood solely as a trans-action between God and individual sinful humans. An im-portant affirmation of any theological anthropology is that we bear the *imago Dei*. All of creation is good but humanity is dif-ferent insofar as we alone are created in God's image. For us as Christians, this means that we bear the image of the triune God, whom we know as Father, Son and Holy Spirit. That image is, of course, marred by our sin. In our brokenness, we seek to re-place the true God with ourselves. And, in doing that, we dis-cover again and again our inadequacy and thus we reveal our shame. Simultaneously, with awareness of that basic inadequacy (acceptance of the serpent's lie of *sicut Deus*) we now expe-rience the other as potential threat. We fear that the other, be that God or neighbor, will discover that we are not who we seek to pretend that we are. We are not *like* God. The other is always a potential judge, one who may see our true selves in all its inadequacy. And even if the other should admire us we fear that eventually the truth will be discovered and we will be abandoned. The loving face will depart and we shall be left alone. And so we hide.

THE TRINITARIAN NATURE OF THE ATONEMENT

The greatest mistakes in theories of atonement occur when the triune nature of God is forgotten. The totality of God intervenes in human history. To fail to recall this forces one into seeing the atonement as something that God does to Jesus. Some theologians have gone so far as to accuse God of child abuse for killing his son. But a trinitarian understanding can spare us from such terrible conclusions. Furthermore, as Jürgen Moltmann has written, the atonement helps us better understand the doctrine of the Trinity. No longer is the Trinity an "exorbitant and impractical speculation about God, but is nothing other than a shorter version of the passion narrative of Christ."[16]

To turn to the Trinity reminds us again of the importance of an incarnational atonement model. The triune God's decision for the Son to take on our humanity is itself atoning. Something profound is accomplished at Christmas as well as on Good Friday and Easter. Each and every day of Jesus' life is a reconciliation of God and humanity. The Sermon on the Mount and each healing act are an offer of forgiveness, an opportunity to repent and believe the good news of the gospel. No doubt, the cross brings a tremendous focus and amplification, as we will examine below. But Jesus' *final* great acts must not be understood as if they alone are his *saving* acts. From Bethlehem to Jerusalem and beyond, God was in Christ, reconciling the world to himself (2 Cor 5:19).

Two points are important before we proceed. First, there is no way to truly plumb the depths of what occurs within the eternal relations among the Father, Son and Holy Spirit. The doctrine of the Trinity remains a mystery before which all our categories eventually fail. Even such important categories as time and space cannot adequately encompass what occurs between Father and Son, Son and Holy Spirit, Holy Spirit and the Father. All analogies eventually limp.

A second point is also important. There is a reason why there are multiple models of atonement. No one theory by itself can completely account for what the Scriptures reveal. As we noted before, the earliest theologians of the church seem to have understood this better than some later practitioners. Thus, what follows is not meant to be the only and true meaning of the atonement. It is merely offered here as another way to begin to explore the depths of God's enduring love for broken humanity. With that in mind, let us begin.

To put it starkly, Father, Son and Holy Spirit, who together are the one God, suffer the death of relationship in shame. Each divine person, in a unique and particular way, enters into the problem of human sin in order to deal with it. Each divine person, in a unique and particular way, experiences the destructive nature of shame in order to vanquish it. As we shall see below when we go into greater detail, the Son is directly shamed, dying the shaming death of the cross. The Father, who has always remained in perfect relationship with the incarnate Son even as he had in eternity, now turns away from the humiliated Son. For the first and only time, there is a break in their relationship. The Holy Spirit, who is the personal relationship between Father and Son, experiences the severing of the relationship. The Spirit is wounded and broken with the impossible distance now separating Father and Son. And it is in this way that shame is taken into the very life of the Trinity. This is no mere transaction between God and humanity. This is the eternal God, Father, Son and Holy Spirit, experiencing and therefore redeeming the heart of human brokenness that is shame. The shame that separates humanity from God, from neighbor and from self-integration is taken up and defeated in the cross.

The truth of God's dealing with shame has been hiding in plain sight all along. It was always there in the passion narrative but we have often failed to perceive it. Our failure of perception has caused us to overlook another possible way to understand Jesus' cry of dereliction; in particular, it may help us understand why Jesus quotes Psalm 22:1 in this terrible moment.[17]

If we could illustrate the way in which the crucifixion provides the moment of shame's undoing it might look something like this. The Son hangs upon the cross; lifted up from the earth, he draws humanity to himself (Jn 12:32). We look on him in his shame and he, looking at us, says, "Father, forgive them; for they do not know what they are doing" (Lk 23:34). Note well: here Jesus uses his unique form of address to God, *Father*. We are drawn to the Father through the Son. On the human side, a restoration has occurred. The relationship that is broken by sin and experienced as shame is healed. We are restored into the perfect loving community that is the divine life of the triune God. The gulf has been spanned and our sins are forgiven.

But in order for this to occur, something else is happening—something that could never be anticipated by us who fear love's durability. Ever and always, Jesus has been in perfect union with God, his Father. The perfection of their relationship has allowed him to go so far as to say, "The Father and I are one" (Jn 10:30). But, now something unimaginable is happening and we only know it because of the cry of dereliction. A shadow has fallen where only sunlight had been. Absence is experienced where only loving presence had been. The Face that never looked away is no longer there. And in that moment Jesus cries out. "And about three o'clock Jesus cried with a loud voice, 'Eli, Eli, lema sabachthani?' that is, 'My God, my God, why have you forsaken me?'" (Mt 27:46).

Even as Jesus faces us, the alienated ones, we who are the shame-filled ones with our *sicut Deus* pretensions, he experiences the brokenness of relationships that shame brings. Faces that turn away are not new to him. Even those closest to him have never fully understood him and thus have never been in complete relationship to him. In various ways, each relative, each acquaintance, each disciple has looked away from him in some way, at some point. And in this last day, he has experienced betrayal, denial and the abandonment of his disciples. But throughout all of this, Jesus has always been sustained by the love of his Father.

The cry of dereliction gives us a glimpse into the inner life of the triune God. Even as the Son experiences the humiliation of his horrible death, the Father turns away. Unable to look at him, there is a break in the communion between Father and Son. At the same time, the Holy Spirit, the personal Spirit common to Father and Son, is broken. The Holy Spirit is wounded. Perhaps Augustine's trinitarian analogy of love may help us here. In turning from the Son, the Father who is the Lover breaks with the Beloved who is the Son. This creates a breach in their Love who is the Holy Spirit. "And if the love whereby the Father loves the Son, and the Son the Father, reveals in an ineffable manner the union between both, what more fitting than that He, who is the Spirit, common to both, should be properly called love?"[18]

Psalm 22:1: "My God, my God, why have you forsaken me? Why are you so far from helping me, from the words of my groaning?"[19] Jesus' use of the psalm reveals an unexpected and dark truth. A true alienation has occurred in that the immediate relationship between Father and Son must now be mediated through the Scripture.[20] This is seen in that the cry of dereliction is the only place where in direct address, Jesus does not call God *Father*. Noting the unique nature of Jesus' addressing God as *Abba*, Joachim Jeremias states, "For only if one takes them (the various Gospel sources) into consideration does a most significant fact become clear: not only do the five strata agree that Jesus did in fact use the address, 'Father,' but they are also at one in making Jesus use this address in *all* his prayers with one exception. The cry from the cross."[21] The cry of dereliction reveals that the Son has lost his direct access to the Father even as he calls out to him as God. He no longer can recognize and thus loses his language, loses the relationship that *Abba* signified. The same one who invited his disciples to share in his relationship with the Father ("When you pray, say: Father, hallowed be your name," Lk 11:2) no longer can see his Father. Is it too much to say that God has become strange to him? Is it possible that at this point, the Son no longer fully knows the Father?

If this is all true—a rupture has occurred in the relationship between the Father and the Son—the Holy Spirit is now also wounded. All three divine persons, each in their own way, experience the breaking of relationship in order that relationship may be restored. None of this is patripassianism or any other denial of the distinct reality of all three persons, because each person experiences shame's breaking power in a unique way: being turned away from, turning away from and the accompanying failure of relationship.[22] Is it any wonder that "darkness came over the whole land" and the "earth shook" (Mt 27:45, 51)?

To grasp fully the significance of Jesus' cry from the cross we must recall again Genesis 3:8-9: "They heard the sound of the LORD God walking in the garden at the time of the evening breeze, and the man and his wife hid themselves from the presence of the LORD God among the trees of the garden. But the LORD God called to the man, and said to him, 'Where are you?'" In the primordial shame experience, God calls to the first Adam, "Where are you?" The first Adam is evasive in his response, betraying the brokenness that sin has brought. In the solution to shame, the second Adam (Rom 5) calls to God, "Where are you?" But this time, it is different because this time it is the loving God who hears and turns again to the Son. How can we be sure of this? How can we know that the breach is repaired? Again, our only clue is what Jesus says: "Then Jesus, crying with a loud voice, said, 'Father, into your hands I commend my spirit.' Having said this, he breathed his last" (Lk 23:46). The relationship is restored and along with it, Jesus' language reveals that special relationship. God has turned his face toward him and the Son once again recognizes his Father. Jesus dies beholding both his Father and his sinful brothers and sisters.[23]

As we have earlier stated, shame *fears* discovery and the accompanying loss of love. The only adequate response to fear is something stronger: "So we have known and believe the love that God has for us. God is love, and those who abide in love abide in God, and God abides in them. Love has been perfected among us in this: that we may have boldness on the day of judgement, because as he is, so are we in this world. There is no fear in love, but perfect love casts out fear" (1 Jn 4:16-18). God who is perfect love overcomes shame's fear. Perfect love has experienced the distancing of relationships and yet has overcome them. And so all those who find their lives united to Christ through the Holy Spirit are given a new place to stand, a place that no longer fears but is given the ability to trust love and therefore love in response.

SHAME AND THE THREE TRADITIONAL MODELS

There are particular ways in which the category of shame reveals greater dimensions to the traditional atonement models. First, with regard to the ransom theory, we recall that the power of the devil is destroyed when he attempts to swallow Jesus into the place of death, not knowing that he has brought the very Lord of life into his realm. In the same way, shame's power, which is the fear of exposure, the fear of the loss of love, is brought into the presence of God. But because this is the One who is love, shame brought into this presence is destroyed; it is rendered powerless. God's power over shame is now shared with all those who are in Christ, with all those who have experienced the depths of shame but now also the love of the Father that will not look away.

The moral influence theory may also be reassessed. In this model, the atonement functions as the greatest example of God's love. When we look upon it, we are transformed, becoming desirous to go and show sacrificial love to others. The category of shame, however, introduces a problem for this model. One critique of the moral influence theory is that it underestimates the depths of human sin. We have no natural desire to look upon the cross or to answer God's call to us. At the same time, however, its emphasis on beholding and contemplating Christ on the cross is significant for facing shame and thus ending its power. Instead of being the moment of atonement, the cross is the magnifying event that reveals what the whole incarnation has been: God's total identification with humanity, including its shame. Shame's power is experienced in the fear of abandonment—the terror of the loss of love. Sinful humanity fears the revelation of the true self, a self that is inadequate, ugly and unlovable. The only solution to that fear is the revelation of the true God, Father, Son and Holy Spirit, that may be beheld in the event of the cross. God is fully revealed as Jesus is fully revealed on the cross. For to see Jesus, to look upon his face, is to behold the Father (Jn 14:9). God, who experiences abandonment and the brokenness of relationship that it implies, is now fully revealed as the One who can be trusted never to abandon anyone. God has experienced the depths of shame: all of its horrible exposure, subsequent abandonment and the loss of relationship. Father, Son and Holy Spirit have experienced shame and have vanquished it, because they do not allow it to destroy their relationship. The Father hears the cry of the Son and turns again. The Son trusts the love of the Father and turns to him. And in that natural turning again, shame loses its power to separate God from humanity.

Perhaps the most difficult model to address is the most prominent one: penal substitution. If penal substitution is understood to be the only biblical or valid theory of the atonement, than the presentation of shame will do little to help. The focus on the courtroom metaphor insists on guilt being the problem. On the other hand, if ultimately the focus is on substitution rather than the way in which Christ substitutes for us, than shame offers a great deal. For there is no doubt, only Jesus fully faced the Father throughout his life. Only he was willing to experience the depths of shame and not turn away from God or his neighbor. He alone could accomplish what no other human had strength or will to do.

Shame's power tends to render us silent. We find it so difficult to face that we do not often speak of it. Instead, we reference our pain and God's loving work in music.

> How deep the Father's love for us,
> How vast beyond all measure
> That He should give His only Son
> To make a wretch His treasure
> How great the pain of searing loss,
> The Father turns His face away
> As wounds which mar the chosen One,
> Bring many sons to glory
> Behold the Man upon a cross,
> My sin upon His shoulders
> Ashamed I hear my mocking voice,
> Call out among the scoffers
> It was my sin that held Him there
> Until it was accomplished
> His dying breath has brought me life
> I know that it is finished
> I will not boast in anything
> No gifts, no power, no wisdom
> But I will boast in Jesus Christ
> His death and resurrection
> Why should I gain from His reward?
> I cannot give an answer
> But this I know with all my heart
> His wounds have paid my ransom

"How Deep the Father's Love for Us" is a beautiful and profound expression of the trinitarian work of the atonement. The divine work, "the searing loss" that rends the divine relationships, brings us all to glory. And in this way our shame is overcome.

So how is this glorious vanquishing of shame applied to us? How do we participate in the triune God's work of atonement? How are our sins forgiven and sin's effects destroyed? It is the face of God revealed in Jesus that gives us the answer.

SIX

"As One from Whom Others Hide Their Faces . . ."

And so now we must explore the way in which Christ's shameful death by crucifixion is redemptive for us. How does Jesus' death on a cross convey healing for shame-filled humanity? New Testament scholar Martin Hengel, in his small yet powerful book *Crucifixion*, has written a concise and masterful account of the Roman practice of crucifixion.[1] It is very important to note that the New Testament insists that the type of death Jesus dies is every bit as important as the fact that he dies. Jesus' public execution through the slow, painful death of crucifixion is central to the New Testament. One of the problems with the traditional atonement models is that they have not offered adequate consideration to the way in which Jesus died. Is there anything added by crucifixion if the main point is that Jesus accepts the death penalty on our behalf, as so emphasized in the penal substitution theory? How does dying on a cross add anything to the defeat of God's enemies as in the ransom theory? Does a dying by crucifixion cause us to understand God's love for us any more than by any other form of execution, as emphasized in the moral influence model? Jesus would have been just as dead by stoning or beheading, two other common means of execution available at the time.

In contrast, the New Testament authors are insistent on the importance of crucifixion as his manner of death. Citing Deuteronomy 21:23, Paul writes, "Christ redeemed us from the curse of the law by becoming a curse for us—for it is written, 'Cursed is everyone who hangs on a tree'" (Gal 3:13). Even here we may observe that Jesus' atoning death goes beyond something that he does to a change in identity. The glorious, sinless one becomes a curse in order to save those who are accursed. Having assumed sinful human nature in the incarnation, the Son of God follows the path of *sicut Deus* humanity to its bitter end. In 1 Corinthians 1:18, Paul writes, "For the message about the cross is foolishness to those who are perishing, but to us who are being saved it is the power of God." There are no parallels in pagan literature to a divine death by crucifixion.[2] Jesus' death on the cross was even scandalous for the early Christians. Hengel observes, "A crucified messiah, son of God or God must have seemed a contradiction in terms to anyone, Jew, Greek, Roman or barbarian, asked to believe such a claim, and it will certainly have been thought offensive and foolish."[3] In other words, Christ's crucifixion achieves a pan-cultural offense and is equally unexpected and unbelievable to all peoples. This is of profound importance. The embracing of the shaming death of crucifixion goes beyond any altruistic or courageous martyrdom. It is an embarrassment, something from which all would naturally look away.[4] And it is for that very reason that we see the cross's power to heal shame.

Furthermore, the evangelical purpose of the New Testament must be remembered. Hengel continues,

> For Paul and his contemporaries the cross of Jesus was not
> a didactic, symbolic or speculative element but a very spe-
> cific and highly offensive matter which imposed a burden
> on the earliest Christian missionary preaching. . . . Pre-
> cisely because of the scandal of the cross, it was impossible
> to be missionary in the ancient world, proclaiming a cru-
> cified messiah and Son of God, without saying something
> about the activity and the death of this man.[5]

Against what must have been the better judgment of a rheto-
rician of Paul's stature, he insists that the way that Jesus dies is
of greater importance than the fact that he dies. In other words,
were the shameful death on a cross not central to Jesus' work,
there would be no possible missional reason to focus on it. Given
both pagan and Jewish thinking, the crucifixion was the primary
counterargument to the early Christian claims regarding the
identity of Jesus Christ.

This is well illustrated by gnosticism in general, but by
Docetism in particular. In Docetism, one may observe an ancient attempt to retain the work of Jesus Christ without the
scandal of the cross. So distasteful is crucifixion to the ancient
pagan mind that an alternative theory was created completely
divorced from the testimony of the eyewitnesses: the Son of God
only appeared to suffer on the cross, but in reality did not. No
respectable deity would ever submit to such an ignoble end.[6]

Hengel summarizes the key points regarding the importance
of Jesus' crucifixion.[7] First, crucifixion was used widely in the
ancient Roman world. Second, it was primarily a political punishment utilized against the lower classes in order to sustain the
Roman status system. But third, it is the very public nature of
crucifixion that is of the greatest significance. Meant to be the

supreme deterrent against challenging Roman authority, it is the public (shaming) nature of the death that is essential. Other deaths may have been more painful, but the slow death of crucifixion emphasized its main lesson: do not challenge Rome. Crucifixion was an efficient means to satisfy the lust for revenge and cruelty, but of even greater importance, "by the public display of a naked victim at a prominent place—at a crossroads, in the theater, on *high ground*, at the place of his crime—crucifixion also represented his uttermost humiliation, which had a numinous dimension to it."[8] The public nature of such an execution invokes the specter of human sacrifice. In this case it is the divine state of Rome that is appeased by the crucified one. Through crucifixion, the Roman state showed its power to maintain peace and restore the status quo. In the light of all this one can better understand what Paul means when he speaks of the folly of the cross.[9]

In light of the meaning of crucifixion, the Western focus on the penal substitution theory presents two primary problems for a pastoral theology of shame and redemption. First, the model's spotlight on human guilt fails to account for the explicit form of Jesus' death: crucifixion. Such a dominant model can lead us to miss the centrality of the meaning of crucifixion. And furthermore, we may fail to realize the "stumbling block" that crucifixion was in telling the story in a missionary context. It was folly to both Jews and Greeks. Second, the Western focus on guilt obscures the core experience of human sin as observed in Genesis and throughout Scripture. What plagues us are not simply our actions or our failure to act in good ways. Instead, our fundamental problem is who we are. And therefore, it is exactly at this point that God insists upon solidarity with sinful humanity—at our most shamed and most impotent state.

It is just at this point that salvation is won and the true glory of God is revealed.

THE SUFFERING SERVANT

Who has believed what we have heard?
And to whom has the arm of the LORD been revealed?
For he grew up before him like a young plant,
and like a root out of dry ground;
he had no form or majesty that we should look at him,
nothing in his appearance that we should desire him.
He was despised and rejected by others;
a man of suffering and acquainted with infirmity;
and as one from whom others hide their faces
he was despised, and we held him of no account. (Is 53:1-3)

Isaiah's "suffering servant" is one of the best-known biblical images. Referring to Mark 14:65, Raymond Brown writes, "In their contemptuous treatment of Jesus as a false prophet, with their spitting and covering his face, and their attendants' slaps, the Sanhedrists are unconsciously fulfilling a prophecy—the great Isaian prophecy revealing that by self-giving, a victim can turn the signs of human rejection into victory through God's help."[10]

The slow, painful death of crucifixion is a public spectacle. Crucifixion is meant to erase all human dignity before the watching eyes of a crowd. It is intended to humiliate as the broken body of the victim twists and contorts in its final attempts to cling to life. Christ's broken body has been the subject of Christian art since the beginning years of the faith. Representations of his death have been the fount of much of our piety. We now turn to one very important aspect of the Lord's broken body: his face.

First, let us note that we are not in need of another atonement model to explore adequately the shame dimensions. We observed above (Col 2:14-15) that shame's power is destroyed by means of Christ's victory. We have also sought to emphasize the fullness of Christ's substitution. His entire life (certainly including his death on the cross) is substitutionary for us. Philippians 2:5-6 reminds us that shame is addressed in Christ's manger beginning. His embrace of humility throughout his life is the truly human way of being. The second Adam need not hide from God behind the mask of pride. Jesus is transparent to his Father and to all those who have eyes to behold him. Finally, the subjective element of the atonement is maintained in that those who will not look away from Christ's shame are empowered to behold the truth of the God who draws near. He comes not to destroy but to save. He does come in judgment but allows the judgment to fall upon himself, and thus all those who look into the dying face of the Savior may see the full revelation of God, the One who knows humanity best and loves them most.

"We live before the faces of others. Some are there physically, others in memory or anticipation." So claims David Ford.[11] This affirmation, which is so essential to Christian faith, may also be observed in what is necessary for basic human development. "Psychological studies show that as early as nine minutes after birth, the child differentiates the face from other patterns. A consistent loving face (usually the mother or primary caregiver) provides the developmental space for the emergence of the child's ego functions, through which she faces the world as a distinct personality."[12] We are born seeking the face of another. Although there is no human face that is always lovingly consistent, everyone needs "good enough" faces in order to develop in a healthy manner.

Therefore, it is in the face of another that we find love and acceptance or hate and rejection. Faces are primary conveyors of what we need to be human. "It is in such face to face meetings, deeply resistant to adequate description, that many of the most significant things in our lives happen, in love and enmity, in education, business, committee meetings, law courts, marriages, families, groups of all sorts."[13] The power of the face is known not only in the present encounter but also in the memory of such encounters. "Imaginatively, we rehearse our lives and intentions before the faces of those we respect, fear, love or otherwise take special notice of or want to impress. What faces do we have habitually in our hearts? Might that be one of the best clues to our identity?"[14]

THE DYING FACE OF CHRIST

In very important ways, our identity is shaped by the faces that we carry with us. At this juncture we may see in a new way the devastating nature of shame—principally signaled by the downturned face. Such are the imagined faces of the shamed that one's own face must look away. All shame strategies are variations on the downturned face.[15] They are all attempts to save face by a refusal to encounter meaningfully the face of another. In Genesis 3 and 4 we have observed how the faces of Adam, Eve and Cain are all turned down and away from interpersonal encounter. By breaking relationship with God, which marks the entrance of sin into reality, the primordial humans encounter a shadow that falls over all relationships. This break in relations is humanity's reorientation from *imago Dei* to *sicut Deus*. *Sicut Deus* is shame-based living. That is, it is the human proclivity to look away from the other and toward the self for the project of identification. We are curved back on ourselves and at the deepest level, we have attempted to become the creators of our own identity.

Human beings live in terror that other faces cannot be trusted. All other faces fail at particular times and particular places to meet the needs of the human ego. This failure is of course a closed loop. Even though we are created to be shaped by other faces, our sinful brokenness fails us in two important ways. First, we have unrealistic expectations. The *sicut Deus* human begins with inflated wants and desires. To be like God is to require more than attention: one deserves worship! And so ultimately no face ever lives up to those sin-based requirements. Second, even as we find the gaze of the other insufficient, we fail to give the other what they need from us. All faces fail, including our own. All love is only temporary, because all is broken by the weight of sin. No face openly offers love in all ways at all times. All faces look away.

The Christian answer to this unsolvable problem is the doctrine of the atonement. The triune God has intervened and done what no mere human can do. To meet God in Jesus Christ is to encounter a face that looks in love and that refuses to look away. But it is a face that one must learn to love, for even though it looks at us lovingly, it is a face that is deeply marred. We are socially conditioned to assume that the beautiful and desirable face will be the one that will answer our needs. Surely it must be that perfect beauty (however measured by any given culture) will have the power to mend human brokenness. But none succeed in accordance with human needs, because all beauty is fading.[16]

And so we must learn to look for another face. We must and may encounter another, unexpected face: a face that redefines beauty.[17] Jesus' is the unexpected face—not one to which we would be naturally drawn. Instead, his is the face from which we would naturally hide our faces (Is 53:3) because it bears the sins of the world and all the shame that such sin bearing must imply. The dying face of Jesus is cloaked in shame and such shame would cause us all to look away. But to yield to that face, to not turn away, is to find life and salvation, for this face has the power to heal because this face belongs to God become human, to Jesus Christ. The fixed, dying gaze of the Savior communicates salvation every bit as much as the divine forgiveness of our guilt pronounced in "Father, forgive them; for they do not know what they are doing" (Lk 23:34). The fixed, dying gaze is the origin point for a new identity, a new way of being human. Or perhaps to state more accurately, the fixed, dying gaze restores to us the old and original way of being human—*imago Dei.*

In the last chapter we listened to Jesus' words from the cross in order to understand how he completely addresses human sin. Jesus dies naked before a watching, sinful world. The man Jesus who fully reveals God is fully revealed before the eyes of all. It is now the precise moment of his death that concerns us. Even as he is breathing his last, there is one more humiliation that awaits him. "After this, when Jesus knew that all was now finished, he said (in order to fulfil the scripture), 'I am thirsty.' A jar full of sour wine was standing there. So they put a sponge full of the wine on a branch of hyssop and held it to his mouth. When Jesus had received the wine, he said, 'It is finished.' Then he bowed his head and gave up his spirit" (Jn 19:28-30). Sinful humanity takes one more opportunity to mock the dying man, giving him vinegar to slake his thirst. It is not his words that now draw our attention, however, but his posture. In dying, Jesus bows his head and he is gone.

In his last act, high and lifted up, Jesus—the man who fully reveals God, now fully revealed—joins sinful humanity in our downward gaze. Jesus dies in the posture of shame, embracing the world's shame. "It is finished." The face, once set like a flint (Is 50:7) on his way to Jerusalem, to this very death (Lk 9:51), now stares unblinkingly downcast, bearing humanity's shame. He joins all of us: solidarity with the shamed. But again, this face is different. For this face in its downward gaze is not looking away from his neighbors; he is looking at them. The last act of the dying Savior is to fix his gaze upon those who are in need of salvation. Our forgiveness has already been pronounced (Lk 23:34) and now the dying God provides the means to accept it. Karl Barth notes that there is no other face like Jesus.'[18] Jesus' is the face that will not look away. Jesus' is the face that sees all and still loves all. Jesus' face alone is the one that has power to forgive and give to us the healing power to accept such forgiveness.

THE RISEN FACE OF THE SAVIOR

If Good Friday were the end of this story we would be left with a tragedy. A wonderful loving man has died, a man who moved toward the shame of others even up to and including his death. But he is still dead. The loving face that will not look away is now placed in a tomb and we see the face no more. As the apostle says, "If Christ has not been raised, your faith is futile and you are still in your sins. Then those also who have died in Christ have perished. If for this life only we have hoped in Christ, we are of all people most to be pitied" (1 Cor 15:17-19). If Friday were the end of the story, we would have the memory of a wonderful man and we would have an example of shame-defying love. But we would not have salvation; we would not have the power to look up from ourselves. But Friday is not the end of the story.

The Father who hears the cries of the second Adam receives him and embraces him. The face lowered on Friday is now lifted up on Sunday. Stripped of all dignity on Friday, he now is robed in glory on Sunday. The face that we avoided because it was too terrible to behold is now seen in the new light of glory. The Gospels are insistent that after his resurrection, Jesus is both recognizable and yet not immediately so. Mary in the garden (Jn 20:11-18) and the disciples on the road to Emmaus (Lk 24:13-35) eventually recognize their risen Lord. The face is familiar, but it takes the disciples a while to comprehend. No doubt, they do not expect to meet him; after all, he is dead! But then again, here he is! Perhaps what causes the initial misapprehension is the new beauty itself. Jesus bears the marks of his shaming (the nail prints, etc.) but with a new glory, a new beauty. Jesus' broken visage now bears a new grandeur. The scars of his brutal and shameful death now reveal the fullness of divine glory. Simultaneously, the crucified Jesus is beheld as the risen Christ.[19] The face from which we would hide our eyes has become the face that attracts us. Jesus' broken face is beautiful, and having met him, we cannot look away from him; we cannot forget him. His beauty calls to us and will not let us go.

The resurrected face of Jesus reveals the finality of God's victory over sin and death. The empty tomb reveals that there is no return to the downturned face. The Father has lifted Christ's face and we are now called to look to him. He is no mere example of a good man. He is the living Lord who has overcome all things that would harm us. His is the face that would not look away, even on Friday, and now we know on Sunday that he never will stop looking.

The resurrection is the vindication of the utterly shamed man, Jesus.

And being found in human form, he humbled himself and
became obedient to the point of death—even death on a
cross. Therefore God also highly exalted him and gave him
the name that is above every name, so that at the name of
Jesus every knee should bend, in heaven and on earth and
under the earth, and every tongue should confess that Jesus
Christ is Lord, to the glory of God the Father. (Phil 2:7-11)

He who had set his "face like flint" was not left in shame because
the one who vindicates is near (Is 50:7-8). The resurrection
shows that shame can be defeated only by being embraced.
Shame is destroyed by turning outward from the self and allowing God to be one's vindication. All other shame strategies
from hiding to lashing out at others are judged and shown to be
ineffectual in Jesus' resurrection. Christ is shown to be victorious in all things, including his embrace of shame.

Furthermore, in the redefinition of beauty, Jesus defeats one
of shame's greatest threats: that we are not fit to be seen. As
Barth points out above, the "beauty" of the resurrected Christ is
a "call" to us. It is a call to let go of our shame-based notions of
what is attractive and what is not. It is a call to allow him to give
us a new identity. That is an identity that does not harbor illu-
sions of the fleeting beauty of youth, but is grounded in a face
(even and especially) broken, yet victorious. The face that will
never look away bears the marks of crucifixion and redefines
beauty. He alone has the power to grant identity to those who
would look to him.

THE ASCENDED FACE OF OUR LORD

Perhaps the most neglected doctrine of the Christian faith is the
ascension of our risen Lord. It would seem to pose a particular

problem for a doctrine of the atonement so dependent on the healing of shame through the face of the risen Savior. Does he still look upon us? How do we see his face if he has returned to the Father? But the opposite is actually the case for the ascension, properly understood, ought to give encouragement to those struggling with forgiveness. As we have already seen, the incarnation is God's movement toward the sinful and shame-filled. The triune God's decision in eternity to not allow humanity to remain broken is the beginning of redemption. There are certainly events in the life of Christ that bring special emphasis. But it must be remembered that Christmas day is as significant for our salvation as Good Friday, Easter Sunday or Ascension Thursday. Ultimately, the incarnation itself is salvific for it is in its totality that sin is addressed.

Central to our understanding of the ascension is that our salvation is not an event located in the past but is the ongoing work of the risen Christ who remains fully human and fully divine. Jesus' ascension moves our faith from the past into the present. This is noted in the Apostles' Creed, wherein Jesus "sitteth at the right hand of the Father."[20] It is the present tense of our salvation that offers us strength and purpose each day. We have been invited to run the good race.

> Therefore, since we are surrounded by so great a cloud of witnesses, let us also lay aside every weight and the sin that clings so closely, and let us run with perseverance the race that is set before us, looking to Jesus the pioneer and perfecter of our faith, who for the sake of the joy that was set before him endured the cross, disregarding its shame, and has taken his seat at the right hand of the throne of God. (Heb 12:1-2)

Christ's ascension reminds us that we may still "look to Jesus" who both continues to face us even as he faces his Father. We look to Jesus who as the "pioneer and perfecter" has both begun and concluded "our faith." What can all this mean except that the work of Jesus continues? Through his ongoing mediation, Christ faces the Father with his resurrected and perfected humanity. In Christ, the Father is pleased and smiles with approval at us. At the same time, the ascended Son of God continues to face us, bringing us forgiveness, healing and full reconciliation with the Father. This is able to happen because the Holy Spirit has come to us and unites us to Jesus. In other words, ever and always, Christ faces both ways: to his Father and to us. The result is our reconciliation and restoration to communion with God.

The ascension reminds us that Christ's humanity, ever before the Father, remains strong even when ours may falter. Our failure to forgive does not stop Christ from forgiving. Our failure to always look to God and neighbor with love does not mean that Jesus ceases to do so. For the Son of God's humanity is a vicarious one. This means that his humanity stands strong in our place, even and especially when we are weak. In recognition of that we are able to join with the apostle Paul and say, "And it is no longer I who live, but it is Christ who lives in me. And the life I now live in the flesh I live by faith in the Son of God, who loved me and gave himself for me" (Gal 2:20). The doctrine of the ascension is an invitation to us to live solely reliant on Christ's ongoing facing and to gain our worthiness solely through him.

Perhaps counterintuitively, it is Christ's ascension (wherein his face seems to be hidden from us) that offers us what we most need in order to turn our faces to each other. In chapter two, we examined Robert Enright's four-phase process for forgiveness. The final phases are meant to create a level of empathy with the offender. "At the beginning of the forgiveness process, the idea of feeling compassion, empathy, or love toward the offender may have been unthinkable, but after a person has decided to forgive and has worked on understanding, a change in feeling is possible."[21] Christians have a resource for empathy unknown to others. The ascended Lord looks upon all with love and continues to both invite and empower us to do the same. We will not do that perfectly, but we are united with the One who does, and so we do not give up, we do not despair. United with the risen and ascended Christ, through the Holy Spirit, we are offered the same mind as Jesus (Phil 2:5). And if we may have the same mind, is it too great a leap to assume that we might have the *same face*? United to Christ, we may see the ones who have hurt us through the eyes of the One who sees perfectly, with the mind that understands completely and with the heart that loves unceasingly.

The ascended face of Christ provides us with the power to forgive in the present, but also reveals the future in which the complete triumph of the triune God will be known. This is seen in Revelation 5 when the slain lamb emerges:

> Then I saw between the throne and the four living creatures and among the elders a Lamb standing as if it had been slaughtered. . . . When he had taken the scroll, the four living creatures and the twenty-four elders fell before the Lamb, each holding a harp and golden bowls full of incense, which are the prayers of the saints. They sing a new song: "You are worthy to take the scroll and to open its seals, for you were slaughtered and by your blood you ransomed for God saints from every tribe and language and people and nation; you have made them to be a kingdom and priests serving our God, and they will reign on earth." (Rev 5:6, 8-10)

He alone is judged worthy to open the scroll. Jesus, the lamb that was slain, the shamed one, is now the only one who reveals true honor and glory. Unlike the suffering of so many innocent victims, Jesus' suffering is not only tragic, it is redemptive. It not only "swells the already overbrimming rivers of blood and tears running through human history,"[22] it answers them. He alone is worthy to reveal the meaning of all the triumphs and tragedies of human history. He alone can stand between the Father and us, reconciling all things. The ascended face of Jesus, who brings us into the presence of the Father, grants us strength to bear the present ambiguities of unforgiven offenses and unreconciled relationships. Such things may be borne in this life with faith because he alone "makes all things new" (Rev 21:5). The perfect humanity of Jesus forgives even when we cannot and reconciles even when we would fear to do so. He is the key to all of the remaining broken places in history. For that reason, it should be no surprise at this point that every creature in heaven and on earth begins to sing (Rev 5:13)! With uplifted faces we may all join the heavenly chorus singing the praises of the one who has vanquished our shame.

SEVEN

LIVING BEFORE CHRIST'S FACE

Jesus told a parable about shame. We don't normally think about it in those terms, but then we don't really like to think in those categories. The parable goes by a number of names, but it is usually called "the prodigal son" (Lk 15:11-32). It is a story about extravagance—riotous living and even more riotous grace. For our purposes, however, it is a story about shame and how it can only be overcome by love. The parable illustrates well the quandary of those who are hiding, those who have forgotten who they really are. It is a parable of grace in that it reveals the reality of the triune God's identity as the one who forgives. The story begins with a shameful incident: the younger of two sons tells his father that he is worth more to him dead than alive. This is an awful thing to say to one's father. It is so awful that it not only brings shame on the son who said it, but also on the family to whom he belongs, and even to the entire village in which he lived. Ancient Palestinian culture had a far greater appreciation of the interconnection of relationships than do we. And so that is a great deal of shame. And then the shameful boy goes off to a far country and loses just about everything, except the memory of his father.

Is it possible that what allows the younger son to come to himself is a memory of his father's face? He comes to himself when he remembers his father and his father's house of plenty. But, of course, the son has not really fully come to himself because he has not adequately remembered his father. He has not seen his father's face for quite some time. He expects judgment but hopes that there might be mercy and that he might be received back as a slave. And so the younger son is still lost even as he makes his way home. Remembering oneself is not salvation. Recognizing one's present difficulty does not change reality. The prodigal cannot yet accept that there is a forgiving Father and so he contrives the servant idea. He is still locked in shame because he cannot yet see the true face of the father. Shame does that: it clouds the memory and causes one to forget love. The son cannot properly see the father, but that does not prevent the father from seeing him (even from a distance!) and so the Father runs to him. Kenneth Bailey points out the great degree of shame activity lying behind that verse.[1] No respectable Palestinian elder runs anywhere; it would be humiliating for him as he hiked up his robe to make the dash toward the son. But so great is the father's love that he embraces shame in order to save the son from the highly likely village welcoming committee who has also been shamed by the son's treatment of the father. Even while being embraced, the son launches into his servant idea. But the father will have none of that. This father wants children, not slaves. And is it possible that in this moment of seeing his father running toward him (running toward shame rather than hiding from it)—is it possible that the son in now hearing the word of grace really begins to remember who he is—not the shaming one who squandered his father's fortune, but the beloved son?

It is important to note that the problem is ultimately not one of spatial distance. The younger son does go into the "distant country," but he had been living in a distant country before he ever actually left his father's house. The conclusion of the parable surprisingly shows that the elder brother is also in a distant country, for he too does not actually live in the facing presence of his father. But the father risks humiliation yet again in leaving the party to go out and plead with the other son (Lk 15:28). Is not this elder brother in the direct line of the first elder brother who also hated his younger brother? Is not this Cain also incapable of knowing where his brother is? He wants him among the dead, among the broken relationships. The parable ends with the elder brother outside, unwilling to look upon the face of a father who could so offend his conscience, a father who could so live outside the elder brother's categories of weak and strong, good and evil. Better to be outside the party than abide the loving face of the one who only desires that we come to ourselves and remember that we are the children of the Father, of the God who forgives.

In this chapter, we want to make some applications. We want to find ways to help one another properly remember (hear and behold) the true God and not some projection of our shame. We want to find ways to help people leave the "distant country" in order to find their home again, having remembered the loving face of the Father, and all their brothers and sisters. We have seen that one of the factors that makes forgiveness difficult is an over-emphasis on guilt rather than shame. There is no doubt that we stand guilty before God as a result of our sins. But we have also observed that the overemphasis on guilt has caused theologians to think of the atonement as an external transaction between God and us. The reasoning goes: God has done something wonderful and now if we would receive it (his loving forgiveness) it is our turn to do something. Penal substitution and moral example both fail when they function as if "the ball is now in our court." They fail to properly stress the true impact of what God has done by taking on human flesh and the ongoing inability of our individual responses to the incarnation. It is the very notion of "our turn now" that is the problem. Such thinking which focuses on our response to God's gracious initiative exacerbates rather than solves our problem. The heart of our problem is on full display at this very point. For those tempted to be like God (*sicut Deus*) our response to God's loving call will always be suspect.

A focus on guilt is also a focus on what we do and have done. And to paraphrase an old adage: to the Christian with a doctrine of penal substitution theory, everything looks like guilt! But it does little to help a person struggling with shame and therefore reinforces our basic problem—falsely believing that we are adequate to restore our relationship with God. Shame-filled people simply do not have the emotional or spiritual strength to deal adequately with their guilt. Until we can come to understand our shame in the light of God's triumph over it, we will make little progress with owning our guilt for our individual sins.

It should come as no surprise that due to its social nature, it is essential that shame be addressed in community. One simply cannot talk themselves out of shame. Shame, per se, is a reflection on how one is being perceived by others. Only the caring and loving faces of others can bring healing to the wounds of shame. Furthermore, as people begin to face Jesus, they begin to gain an awareness of others. As we look up from our shamed, sinful selves we see that Jesus' loving gaze is strong enough to hold us and countless others at the same time. Looking up from ourselves we not only see the Lord, but we begin to perceive our neighbor in a correct manner. To turn our eyes upon Jesus brings not only our individual healing but a responsibility to help others return the Lord's loving gaze. David Ford writes, "This too involves abundant particularity, recognizing the face of Christ as reflected in all the faces to which (even when they are not aware of it) he relates. It also involves infinite responsibility, as the face of Christ to which believers turn directs them (if they understand rightly to whom they are looking) to those on whom he looks with love."[2]

To behold oneself in the eyes of Christ is salvation. To lock eyes with Christ further implies openness to beholding everyone else upon whom he looks. This is the ethical implication of salvation; this is the mandate to forgive even as we are forgiven. We never cease looking at Christ's face of love. But looking at his face causes us to behold all the others upon whom he also looks. It causes us to move toward shame and not away from it, just like the father in Jesus' parable, just like Jesus himself.

Helmut Thielicke observes something similar:

> I find it impossible to be afraid to say: Rather a worm in the eyes of Jesus than a god in the eyes of men! That's why it is the eyes of Jesus Christ that hold the world together, for they give us men a totally new relationship to one another. From this, however, it follows quite simply that now we must put ourselves beneath these eyes. . . . One cannot "love" someone simply at command or forgive him or have respect for the life and property of another . . . simply because one is commanded to do so. I can do all this only if I stand in the discipleship of this Lord and see the world, my country, my neighbor through his eyes.[3]

In that "the eyes of Jesus Christ hold the world together" we are called to live differently. We are called to view others so that they might receive Christ's gaze of love and in turn share that with others. Ultimately, only this produces the empathy necessary for Christian forgiveness: one sinner recognizes another sinner through the eyes of Christ.

HELPING EACH OTHER FACE CHRIST

In Christian community we may help one another face Christ in a number of ways. In one sense these are simply the spiritual disciplines necessary to wean us away from insisting that conscience be our guide. We have already discovered the ambiguity of conscience. It may not lead us closer to the truth of our lives, but actually further from it. From Bonhoeffer we have learned that conscience itself may be one of the primary ways in which we hide from the God who loves us. In response, we need to help people replace the "voice" of conscience with the "face" of conscience.

Christians are the people who have in faith yielded their lives to Jesus Christ. For our purposes here, this means that of all the faces we encounter, whether they are presently seen or remembered, only one has authority over us. That is the face of Jesus. Christians are the people who seek to live their lives before the face of Jesus. We have come to believe that only Jesus sees us properly. Only Jesus has authority to grant us our true honor and identity. Only Jesus continues to stand between us and his Father, praying for us and substituting for us. In no other eyes may we see our faces correctly reflected. All other faces look away, so all other faces fail. It is too great a burden for any of us to give to another what the other truly needs. None of us (at least in this life) have the ability to love fully and completely at all times and in all situations. The mutual recognition of this deficit is actually an important step toward better loving and forgiving. Christians have the luxury of allowing one another to fail, knowing that there is One who never fails. In the light of this, it is important to acknowledge that all other faces, be they shaming or loving, cannot be trusted with total devotion. Only one may be worshiped: the face of Jesus.

At the same time, we are in desperate need of one another to help us see Jesus. Christian communities are places meant to remind us of Jesus' face and how to live before his lovingly watchful eyes. They are places that help us learn what Greg Jones calls the "craft of forgiveness."[4] They are places where we find our own healing in ministering to the needs of others. Christian communities are meant to be the "safe places" where we learn how to accept forgiveness even as we offer it to others. They are meant to be places of hospitality and acceptance.

But that is easier said than done. All too often our communities fail in welcoming others and in helping others behold the open and welcoming face of Christ. Fearful that love is a "zero-sum game" we worry that others will divert Christ's gaze away from ourselves. And so we are tempted to see the church as only for us and a few others who are like us. Or we may fall into the opposite trap of settling for an all-too-human form of acceptance. This is an acceptance that allows us to continue to abide in shame-filled identities by agreeing not to challenge one another. We may work together in such communities but without ever making the type of eye contact necessary for true transformation.

Instead, communities that help one another live before the face of Christ will be places where the office of the keys (Mt 16:19) is administered. Christ has chosen to exercise his authority through redeemed sinners and so we all need the "binding and loosing" of our brothers and sisters in order not to settle for other faces. We are only too willing to return to

old shame-filled identities and so we all need particular disciplines for shame-free living. Christian discipline, properly
practiced, is never meant to be a way of separating sheep from
goats, but always a path of helping a lost sheep return home.
In Matthew 25:31-46, only the Son of Man has authority to
separate the sheep from the goats. That is never our work;
such separation can only belong to the One who loves perfectly and completely. Christian communities that practice
loving discipline never lose sight that all are ever and always
sinners saved by grace.

Robert Karen, in his foundational essay on shame, looks back
wistfully to a lost era:

> In medieval Christendom the belief that all people were
> sinners, that all were unworthy, used this sense of uni-
> versal defect to bind the community, to maintain a spir-
> itual focus, and perhaps incidentally, to drain off some
> shame that might otherwise have become individual and
> narcissistic. From our distant perspective in a diametri-
> cally different world, we can easily imagine how com-
> forting it might have been to know that one was not alone
> in one's flaws and vulnerabilities, to feel assured of one's
> place despite everything, to be confident that all were
> equal in God's eyes.[5]

It is a judgment on the contemporary church that Karen believes
such communities belong to a long past era. It is a challenge to
the church today through the power of the Holy Spirit to build
again such communities that the world may yet believe that
Jesus Christ has the power to forgive sin, healing all guilt and
shame. This is possible as we rest confident that God does love
us and is sufficient for all our needs.

NECESSARY PRACTICES FOR LIVING
BEFORE JESUS' FACE: (1) CONFESSION

At the conclusion of *Dead Man Walking*, Sister Helen Prejean says to condemned murderer Matthew Poncelet, "I want the last face you see in this world to be the face of love, so you look at me when they do this thing. I'll be the face of love for you." Perhaps without fully understanding what she is doing, by showing love to Matthew (a very unlovable character), Sr. Helen is able to address Matthew's shame. This is the essential overture that will ultimately enable him to own his guilt in the grisly murder of two teenagers. Only her loving care for him as his spiritual advisor allows him the place to stand so that he may own his guilt. Such significant work requires a willingness to hear difficult things and to provide the face that mirrors Jesus' face who looks in love at even those who have done terrible things.

Many Protestants struggle with the idea that anyone needs anyone else in order to confess their sins. One might go so far as to say that a basic part of the DNA structure of Protestantism is the belief that no additional mediator is necessary to stand between oneself and God. After all, did not the Reformation occur for exactly that purpose? What does the "priesthood of all believers" mean after all? Is not everyone able to go directly to God with all their worries, grief and sins? Well, on the one hand, of course that is correct. As the old saying goes, "The ground is level at the foot of the cross." There is no point of higher ground where one can stand above other believers. No person has better access than another to the Lord.

On the other hand, all of us are marked by the shame that predisposes us to a weakness of vision. Thus all of us at some point need help. God in his mysterious wisdom has chosen others afflicted with the same weakness of vision to help in what might be called "ministries of pointing." We are all called to point to Christ even as did John the baptizer (Jn 1:29-34). Letting go of our need to prove ourselves, we are able to join John in affirming that Jesus must increase while we decrease (Jn 3:30). In living before Christ's face, from time to time, all Christians are called to be the face of love for others. All of us are called to reflect Christ's beautiful face. Having seen that face ourselves, we perceive that he looks at others even as he looks at us. And so like him, we also turn our attention out to them.

A renewed practice of the confession of sins of one Christian to another would help many come to understand that one of our greatest needs is to have a trusted "brother" or "sister" in whom we may confide our deepest points of sorrow and failure. Bonhoeffer writes, "We do not understand sin through our experience of life or world, but rather through our knowledge of the cross of Christ. The most experienced observer of humanity knows less of the human heart than the Christian who lives at the foot of the cross of Christ. No psychology knows that people perish only through sin and are saved only through the cross of Christ."[6]

As helpful as therapy can be, there remains a profound difference between the therapist-client relationship and the relationship between two Christians who are both looking at the face of Jesus. Bonhoeffer goes on to affirm that once a person sees the profundity of their own sins, they can never really be shocked again by the sins of another. Most importantly, what is essential for Bonhoeffer (as we have seen with others) is that a true knowledge of sin can only be acquired within the larger context of God's remarkable intervention and forgiveness. Proper confession may only follow a proper affirmation of God's remarkable grace. "The spirit of judgment is cut off at the roots. He knows the other to be accepted by God in the midst of his lostness even as he is accepted. He loves brother and sister under the cross."[7]

MAX THURIAN AND PROTESTANT CONFESSION

Max Thurian's classic work, *Confession*, is a powerful corrective to Protestant misgivings regarding our need for each other in confessing our sins "properly."[8] It is certainly the case that many traditions understand the ordained to have a particular role in a ministry of confession. But they are not the only ones who may perform this significant ministry. Anyone who has beheld Christ's face has become an apostle of that face. And as an apostle, all bear a vocation to help others see him.

The old tradition of confession certainly sees a particular form of that activity as integral, but not essential. Such acts as contrition and confession are very important but only absolution is essential.[9] As a matter of fact, any practice that places too much focus on "proper" sorrow for sin is always misguided because our sorrow, not grounded in Jesus' face of love, is always malformed by sin. Any act of confession that does not begin with Christ ends as some form of "plea bargaining" in which we plead guilty to lesser charges. Only a true vision of Christ can inspire a true vision of oneself. Therefore, above all else, hearing the good news of forgiveness is the one indispensable thing in confession. In other words, to go to confession is always about the proper receiving (hearing one's forgiveness) rather than a proper giving (sorrow, full account of sin, etc.).[10]

There is no doubt; such practices can lead to "cheap grace" wherein a person comes to believe that God is weak and indulgent.[11] Such people may continue to expect forgiveness without really acknowledging Christ's look of love. Still, as in the parable of the prodigal, the Father does not ask his servants for their opinion regarding his lavish love for the once lost but now found son. He only instructs us to bring signs of complete acceptance: "But the father said to his slaves, 'Quickly, bring out a robe—the best one—and put it on him; put a ring on his finger and sandals on his feet. And get the fatted calf and kill it, and let us eat and celebrate; for this son of mine was dead and is alive again; he was lost and is found!' And they began to celebrate" (Lk 15:22-24). This may well be one of the church's most common points of failure: we would balk at the lavishness of God's favor. Perhaps we continue to fear that too much love, too much forgiveness for another places our own love and forgiveness in jeopardy.

Thurian also helps us understand that the fount of authority for absolution never comes from the perfection of the one who hears a confession. It is just the opposite. One's "own experience of sin and forgiveness can inspire . . . greater compassion and gentleness of heart."[12] We are never empowered to hear confessions by our own obedience and faithfulness but by our own willingness to appropriate God's forgiveness and by our own willingness to behold Christ's face.[13] To properly hear the confession of another, one must first remember Christ's face, looking on with compassion through his eyes, hearing the brokenness of another with his ears and speaking gently, yet firmly with his mouth, "Neither do I condemn you. Go your way, and from now on do not sin again" (Jn 8:11).

Finally, Thurian reminds us that one's posture is important. One ought not to stand over another person, but kneel together with him or her.[14] This then leaves no doubt of the equality of all before Christ. There is never any graduation from this ultimate dependence on God's gracious word of absolution. Christ's word of forgiveness sets the prisoner free and is also a summons to go forth for those who have heard it for themselves. Thus the word of absolution both offers comfort and a call to action. All who hear, "Your sins are forgiven" are given authority to tell others the same good news

Confession brings healing when the shame of one's sin is exposed to another. "There are things which, when put into words, lose their evil attraction, so that the more one speaks of them the less desire one has to do them. . . . As long as men still cast a veil of mystery over some sinful propensity in their natures, they enhance its power to tempt them and increase the attraction the sin has for them."[15]

Every experience of confession will be unique. There are no exact scripts to follow and no particular places that are better than others. A confession at the bar rail in the tavern may be just as effective as at the communion rail in the cathedral. Still, as unique as each confession will be, there are certain things they must have in common. Eduard Thurneysen enumerates five marks of true confession.[16] First, there is a confident assurance that the person who makes confession will be forgiven. Nothing else is possible if that is not the foundation of the practice. Second, absolution must be specific and explicit. Jesus does not forgive us our sins in general, but he forgives the particulars, no matter how ashamed of them one may be. Third, since it is God who forgives, the practice of confession ought to begin and end with the reading of Scripture. Forgiveness is not the Christian's good news; it is not based on the authority of anyone else's life. It is good news precisely because it is God's word to us. Fourth, as in Jesus' words to the woman caught in adultery, admonition follows pardon.

The test of genuine pastoral conversation will be admonition without any compulsion to perfectionistic, oppressive deeds of obedience, or to self-fulfillment of the law. . . . In an uninterrupted sequence of vital acts, he will take up the fight, unceasingly recognizing himself as a sinner, yet as a sinner fortunate enough to know his sin attacked, indeed conquered by forgiveness.[17]

Finally, confession is meant to lead to the fellowship of others who have heard the good news of forgiveness, who have beheld Christ's loving face. None have the strength to "go and sin no more" left to themselves. We go together in order to sin no more. All are meant to seek the company of other sinners saved by grace. There the good work may continue. Confession is a self-revelation. It is a stripping away of one's excuses, leaving oneself exposed before the eyes of the other. Confession is the recognition that all our excuses have not been able to hide the truth of our lives. And so confession makes us naked before the eyes of the other. But having become naked—that is, realizing the truth of our nakedness—we are also provided the place to put on Christ. Unlike the temporary garments of skin provided to Adam and Eve (Gen 3:21), being clothed in Christ grants a new identity.

With the revealing of sin to another, strength is given to put on Christ (Rom 13:14). In giving away the "veil of mystery," one discovers that one's nakedness is clothed by Jesus Christ himself. George Herbert said it very well in "The Dawning":[18]

Awake sad heart, whom sorrow ever drowns;
Take up thine eyes, which feed on earth;
Unfold thy forehead gather'd into frowns:
Thy Saviour comes, and with him mirth:
Awake, awake;

And with a thankfull heart his comforts take.
But thou dost still lament, and pine, and crie;
And feel his death, but not his victorie.
Arise sad heart; if thou dost not withstand,
Christ's resurrection thine may be:
Do not by hanging down break from the hand,
Which as it riseth, raiseth thee:
Arise, Arise;
And with his buriall-linen drie thine eyes:
Christ left his grave-clothes, that we might, when grief
Draws tears, or bloud, not want an handkerchief.

The little detail of the left-behind grave clothes (Jn 20:5-7) has fascinated exegetes since the earliest days of the church. The traditional interpretation understood the shroud and face covering to be a proof of the resurrection. Reformers such as Calvin used the text as a polemic against certain Catholic pieties, such as the shroud of Turin and Monica's veil. But for our purposes, the text may serve as a reminder to us that as we allow our eyes to rise from our brokenness in order to behold the resurrected Lord, we can be stripped of our shame and our many ineffective attempts to cover our nakedness. We need no longer live in "garments of skins" (Gen 3:21). They were never meant to be anything other than a temporary solution offered as a measure of mercy. Jesus leaves behind him the things of death. By confessing our sins to another, we too may leave behind the tattered rags in which we have lived. To confess and to know our sins forgiven is to put on Christ in his glory. With our eyes lifted to him, we may also leave the tombs of our resentment and fear. In doing so, we may come to understand and affirm the words of Charles Williams: "But forgiveness is the resolution of all into a kind of comedy, the happiness of reconciliation, the peace of love."[19] Perhaps for the first time, we may affirm that all truly is well that ends well.

NECESSARY PRACTICES FOR LIVING BEFORE JESUS' FACE: (2) SMALL GROUPS

In life together with other believers we begin to think beyond our own need for forgiveness and reach out to others. It is within small groups that we now gain a greater vision that Christ not only looks upon us in love, but he also holds countless others in his loving gaze. Unlike us, Christ is able to love all completely and fully. Unlike us, Christ gives himself completely to any and all. It is within small gatherings of those who are learning to face Jesus that we also begin to gain Christ's vision.

The early Methodist bands provide an excellent example of how such group work might occur today. Pastoral theologian Ed Wimberly has observed, "There is no doubt that the Wesleyan heritage of the practice of conversation must be a central element in responding to the presence of psychological shame. . . . The dominant fear of being unloved and thus worthless confirms human beings' lack of identity, and the only way human beings are affirmed is in relationship with others, and with God. It is group conversation that provides this element."[20]

We are well aware of support groups that are designed to meet various human needs. Many churches have these groups aimed at issues like grief support, divorce recovery, dementia support, addiction recovery and so on. But few churches have the sort of small groups that were the hallmark of early Methodism. John Wesley, its founder, recounts the beginning of small groups that were central to the Methodist movement: "By the blessing of God upon their endeavors to help one another, many found the pearl of great price. . . . These felt a more tender affection than before to those who were partakers of like precious faith; and hence arose such a confidence in each other that they poured out their souls into each other's bosom."[21] The early Methodists, finding God's forgiveness and acceptance, began to connect with one another in a new and powerful way. A natural affinity grew among those who had beheld the loving face of Christ. "Indeed they had great need so to do; for the war was not over, as they had supposed. But they had still to wrestle both with flesh and blood, and with principalities and powers; so that temptations were on every side; and often temptations of such a kind as they knew not how to speak in a class, in which persons of every sort, young and old, men and women, met together."[22]

Here was born the Methodist focus on being "made perfect in love." This is the particular way in which they came to describe God's ongoing work of sanctification. Beholding Christ's face had begun a process of learning how to live consistently before his face. "These therefore wanted some means of closer union: they wanted to pour out their hearts without reserve, particularly with regard to the sin which did still 'easily beset' them, and the temptations which were most apt to prevail over them. . . . In compliance with their desire I divided them into small companies; putting married or single men, and married or single women together."[23] And so John Wesley imparted his great gift to the Christian movement: a way to organize believers so as to maximize their response to God's ongoing work.

In this way, John Wesley stumbled into the genius of Methodism: an organizational plan that allowed for the types of conversation necessary for the path of sanctification. The "war was not over" with an initial knowledge of God's forgiveness. There needed to be a way to address the human brokenness that re-mained. It needs to be noted that the conversation of the "bands" focused on issues of guilt. These five questions were asked at every meeting:

1. What known sins have you committed since our last meeting?

2. What temptations have you met with?

3. How were you delivered?

4. What have you thought, said, or done, of which you doubt whether it be sin or not?

5. Have you nothing that you desire to keep secret?[24]

Specific to behavior, the questions were meant to encourage an honest engagement with particular sins that continued to trouble believers postconversion. The forgiveness of guilt guided the conversation, but the fifth question and the structure of the group itself addressed shame. By requiring open conversation in small Christian groups (usually five to six people), Wesley enabled the early Methodists to realize that they were not the only Christians who struggled as disciples. The leader of the group always went first in describing their struggles and failures. The fifth question directly addressed broken attempts to hide and not expose the true self. As noted above, the groups were segregated according to gender and marital status. That structure was meant to allow for a more honest and vulnerable conversation. Shame is difficult enough to expose without the added issues that mixed groups would foster. Promoting an environment of loving care, the early Methodists found relief from both guilt and shame. Such honesty allowed them to move from a condemning conscience to "godly sorrow."[25]

How might such groups function today? They have their parallels in twelve-step groups. Perhaps in many churches, the most honest engagement with issues of shame does not happen on Sunday morning in the sanctuary but on Saturday night in the small meeting room. The mutual recognition of need and brokenness allows a conversation that goes beyond categories of winners and losers, of those who are "in" and those who are "out." At the same time, Christian shame groups could also move past the sense of "self-help" that therapeutic culture fosters. Insofar as the face of Jesus alone has power to heal shame, intentional Christian groups can address shame in a way that goes beyond the twelve-step focus on a "higher power." The essential problem with a "higher power" is that such ambiguity plays into our primordial fear of the God who approaches us. Left to our own imaginations, we lack the ability to envision properly the face of the God who is sufficient to reach our deepest needs. We need to know and face the true God if we would honestly face the truth of our lives. The face of Jesus reveals both the fullness of God and the fullness of humanity. No wonder then that included among the verses of the great acclamation of early Methodist faith is the following: "Jesus! The name that charms our fears, that bids our sorrows cease; 'tis music in the sinner's ears, 'tis life, and health, and peace."[26]

Such groups, just as were the early Methodist bands, must not be mandatory. One cannot force this type of intimate conversation. However, one would hope that as word began to circulate of the help discovered through such a process, people would earnestly desire to join one. One can only try, making space for God's graciousness.

NECESSARY PRACTICES FOR LIVING
BEFORE JESUS' FACE: (3) WORSHIP

Called upon to mediate Christ's forgiving face one to another in both one-on-one and small group settings, we are prepared for community, and particularly for the hallmark of Christian community: worship of the triune God. And yet so much of our worship is self-centered. At best we often come to the assembly of the saints in order to "get our batteries charged." We do this knowing that there is something missing in life, something that we need. At worst, we gather with other Christians in order to be entertained or at least diverted from all the drudgery of life. We think to ourselves, "Meet my immediate needs or else I will find some other church with better music or better youth ministry or better coffee!" As long as we gather together focused on ourselves, we will miss what might really happen as we offer all praise to the triune God. We will miss what we need most when we remain so utterly focused on what we think we need.

"For I am not ashamed of the gospel; it is the power of God for salvation to everyone who has faith, to the Jew first and also to the Greek" (Rom 1:16). Allowing God to refocus our lives from ourselves to him strengthens us. It continues the process of our healing. It allows shame, which has been defeated, to remain defeated for us. The key is to allow Jesus to be the criterion of all that we value and all that we would honor. Writing to the Corinthians, Paul says,

> Consider your own call, brothers and sisters: not many of you were wise by human standards, not many were powerful, not many were of noble birth. But God chose what is foolish in the world to shame the wise; God chose what is weak in the world to shame the strong;

> God chose what is low and despised in the world, things
> that are not, to reduce to nothing things that are, so that
> no one might boast in the presence of God. He is the
> source of your life in Christ Jesus, who became for us
> wisdom from God, and righteousness and sanctification
> and redemption, in order that, as it is written, "Let the
> one who boasts, boast in the Lord." (1 Cor 1:26-31)

Boasting about oneself is often indicative of a shame defense
strategy. That is, we speak well of ourselves for fear that no one
else will. But Paul invites us to no longer do that, but instead to
boast of the Lord, the one who has brought us from nothing to
everything. Worship, therefore, should be focused on such
boasting, on giving honor to the one who fully embraced shame.
This is no longer a defense strategy on our part. Most of us are
quite adept at boasting. For instance, we brag about our children
on bumper stickers: "My child is an honor student at . . ." Our
vehicles of transportation have become conveyors of our fragile
egos as well as our bodies.[27] This therefore is a new thing: to
boast of Christ's victory implies an ongoing surrender of our
own attempts at saving ourselves, our vain efforts at managing
our own shame.

As we saw at the conclusion of the last chapter, in Revelation
5, our praise is only able to join the heavenly chorus when the
Lamb appears, who still bears the marks of his shaming death.
Then and only then are we able to see beyond all our failed attempts at self-preservation. The worship of God is a glorious gift
of God to us, even as we sing God's praises. Losing ourselves in
"boasting of the Lord" gives us power to raise our faces and be
set free of all things that restrain us from the abundant life that
Christ offers.

Understanding worship as the focal point in which we cease boasting of ourselves and boast only of Christ allows us to better understand several aspects of traditional worship. First, as we have already examined, a call to confession is principally another way in which the gospel is proclaimed and Christ's victory is celebrated. In the call to confession, there should not be one iota of doubt that Jesus Christ forgives us our sins. Unfortunately, Christians often act as if their forgiveness depends on remembering all their sins or feeling appropriately sorry for them. Most of us, of course, have much for which we ought to feel sorry! But that is not the point. Instead the call to confession ought to acknowledge the overarching reality that we have not been left alone in our shame. We are a privileged people who may confess with all honesty because we have come to know that "the Son of Man came to seek out and to save the lost" (Lk 19:10). The call to confession ought to be one of the most celebrated and joyfully anticipated moments in worship. For this is the point in which we are reminded not so much about how we have sinned, but about the God who has relentlessly sought us out and has found us. The call to confession ought to be the point in the week in which we are most aware of the reality that the depths of our sin have been overcome by the far greater depths of God's passionate love.

Worship as a communal discipline offers a unique venue for one sinner to admit the reality of their lives in the company of other sinners. Confession in worship is primarily the community recognizing its ongoing need for forgiveness. It is the unique reorientation of those who have already responded to the gospel and a reminder of their ongoing need for grace. Communal confession ought to disabuse all Christian communities of the shame-based notion that they are somehow better than those who have not heard the good news of Jesus. Such confession then is meant to remind us of our need to share this good news with others who are still hiding from God. We seek forgiveness that in our failure to boast only of the Lord, we have obscured the clarity of God's good news. Communal confession as a weekly event offers the reality check necessary for humbly following the Lord who alone defines humility. Communal confession, rather than an opportunity to wallow in remorse, is meant to be a reminder to us of God's gracious initiative and our call as a new people to go forth and proclaim it.

Finally, regarding confession as an aspect of worship, it is important to recall that we are not only acknowledging our individual sins, but also confessing the corporate sins of the church. Together, we have failed to boast of Christ. Together, we have ignored the poor and the sick and the imprisoned. We have failed as community because of our shame, which has debilitated our power to be honest with one another. Communal confession is meant to reverse that failure.

THE LORD'S PRAYER

Christian worship also provides us an opportunity to be mindful of our individual sins. Most Christians when gathered together pray the Lord's Prayer. "He was praying in a certain place, and after he had finished, one of his disciples said to him, 'Lord, teach us to pray, as John taught his disciples'" (Lk 11:1). Praying Jesus' prayer is our ongoing recognition that we do not of ourselves have words that are sufficient to address God. We just don't know where to start! And so Jesus graciously invites us *to pray as he prays*. Most importantly, the Lord's Prayer is more than a formula for what constitutes a correct prayer. It is again a reorientation for us. It is an invitation to address God in the same way that Jesus addresses God.

To pray "Our Father" is a sign that we have been empowered
by God the Son, through God the Holy Spirit, to properly recognize God who is our Father. That we may address God as
Father puts everything else in proper context. In praying Jesus'
prayer we share in his relationship with the Father. We are empowered to recognize God for who he truly is, the loving Father
who goes forth to meet his wayward children. Everything else in
the prayer must and can only be prayed with that image in mind.
This is the God who approaches us with love.

This is particularly true for the phrase that sometimes bothers
Christians: "Forgive us our sins [debts/trespasses], for we ourselves
forgive everyone indebted to us" (Lk 11:4). If we are going to take
seriously the reality of God's reconciling love, then we dare not
read some form of contingency into the relationship between our
receiving and offering forgiveness. In other words, we cannot at
this point return to our speculations regarding an "unknown God"
who waits to act or love or forgive until we have done our part. To
hypothesize like that is to renounce the status that the Father's only
Son has granted us in relationship to him. Such contingencies are
foreign to all that we know of God through Jesus.

Having said that, there still is a relationship between receiving
and offering forgiveness. It is a relationship to which Jesus refers
elsewhere. The parable of the unforgiving servant in Matthew 18
is a stark reminder that we who have been forgiven are called
upon to forgive. But our forgiveness always comes first. It is the
place wherein we stand. One way to understand it is that we
receive forgiveness with the same hand by which we offer it to
others. It is impossible to live in our new status as the children
of God if we are unwilling to forgive others.

But it is also at exactly this point that we must remember
that Jesus has not left us merely an example of forgiveness to

follow. Jesus Christ has ascended and he continues to pray for us, mediating our broken, unforgiving humanity to his Father. In his vicarious humanity, he continues to present us in himself to the Father in his ongoing self-offering. And our great High Priest is especially aware of how difficult forgiveness is and so he prays for us. The reality of Christ's ongoing work is never a call for us to give in or give up. Instead, ever and always, it is the call to persevere and to never doubt the depths of God's love for us. Our praying of the prayer that Jesus taught us is always a joining of the Lord in his ongoing prayer. We can only pray because he always prays. Austin Farrer described the predicament of our praying:

> It is nearly impossible to pray, but the overcoming of that impossibility, that is just what prayer is. If you could pray when you set yourself to pray, then perhaps you would not need to pray. . . . Nevertheless, pray in your insincerity, until your prayers cease to be your prayers alone, until the sun of God's charity has warmed you into life, and turned your heart of stone into a heart of flesh.[28]

Our prayers are never effective by themselves. Perhaps our prayers are even insincere much of the time. But are prayers (even if ineffective or insincere) are never alone, for Christ prays for us and with us. Commenting on Romans 8:26 ("Likewise the Spirit helps us in our weakness; for we do not know how to pray as we ought, but that very Spirit intercedes with sighs too deep for words"), Barth reminds us, "The justification of our prayer and the reality of our communion with God are grounded upon the truth that Another, the Second Man from Heaven (I Cor. XV. 47), stands before God pre-eminent in power and—in our place."[29] In his praying with and for us, we join the unending hymn of praise to him that continues to resound in heaven: "Then I heard every creature in heaven and on earth and under the earth and in the sea, and all that is in them, singing, 'To the one seated on the throne and to the Lamb be blessing and honor and glory and might forever and ever!'" (Rev 5:13).

EXPERIENCING THE DEFEAT OF SHAME

Those who have beheld Jesus' face, those who have begun to see the others at whom Christ gazes in love, are experiencing their healing through the defeat of shame. They understand their own honor and value in Christ and are gaining the strength to see and be seen by others. In this way, God calls to his children to come out from hiding and have fellowship with him. In answering that call, we move from a *sicut Deus* to an *imago Dei* identity. Just how much healing may we expect in this life? In other words, does the atonement—does God's facing of us in Jesus Christ— offer any specific answer to the core problems of human identity? Specifically, may we expect any answer to the broken relationships that we experience in our work and our love? Let us return to the beginning, for it is there that these two problem areas are highlighted.

> To the woman he said, "I will greatly increase your pangs in childbearing; in pain you shall bring forth children, yet your desire shall be for your husband, and he shall rule over you." And to the man he said, "Because you have listened to the voice of your wife, and have eaten of the tree about which I commanded you, 'You shall not eat of it,' cursed is the ground because of you; in toil you shall eat of it all the days of your life; thorns and thistles it shall bring forth for you; and you shall eat the plants of the field. By the sweat

of your face you shall eat bread until you return to the
ground, for out of it you were taken; you are dust, and to
dust you shall return." (Gen 3:16-19)

In these verses, God speaks the consequences of *sicut Deus*
living; God foretells of the alienation that is the necessary
outcome of shame-based living. Our relationships to work and
to those we love have become broken. Genesis 3:17-19 shows
that our relationship to labor is broken by sin. Genesis 2:15
("The LORD God took the man and put him in the garden of
Eden to till it and keep it") speaks of work with purpose insti-
tuted by God. This is vocation. The good may be known and
increased through work, but it cannot constitute identity. Few
in the modern economy experience work in that way. Instead,
work becomes an all-out pursuit of money. For many, money is
the sole motivation for work because so many people do not
enjoy their work. Gallop frequently surveys people to discover
the level of work satisfaction. Barry Schwartz notes, "Its survey
last year found that almost 90 percent of workers were either
'not engaged' with or 'actively disengaged' from their jobs. Think
about that: nine out of ten workers spend half their waking lives
doing things they don't really want to do in places they don't
particularly want to be."[30] When joy is only discovered in the
paycheck at the conclusion of the work, money takes on too
great a place in one's life. Such an ongoing quest for money and
the things that it buys becomes one of the primary ways in
which we continue to hide from God and others. This is seen in
that money's power is ultimately related to status; it would give
us value that we otherwise find lacking in the self. It is a straightforward measurement of value in which it is easy to pick
winners and losers. All that is needed is an answer to the

question, "How much are they worth?" In this way, the poor are forgotten, written off as unknown others who do not work hard enough to earn a good living.

Earning money is not wrong in itself. Furthermore, the problem is not in the amount that one earns. Instead, money becomes an idol. It becomes the means by which we measure value. It becomes a primary way of the vain pursuit of *sicut Deus*. Money's pursuit all too often is one of our greatest shame management strategies. And in the end, no amount of money, no car so expensive or house so large is able to satisfy shame's ache. Ultimately, the pursuit of money absent vocation alienates one from joy, from a greater purpose in work.

But for those who have beheld the face that does not look away, the joy of vocation may be discovered. It may be discovered because work can once again take its rightful place in life. It no longer need be the source of identity. In joyful work, the self is displaced from the center of attention and self-forgetfulness occurs. In this sense, self-forgetfulness is actually seeing the created self correctly. It is neither self-denigration nor self-aggrandizement, two ineffective shame alleviation strategies. Other workers are seen differently. Employers and employees need not be seen as enemies but as colaborers working together with purpose. Differences will remain, but they need not be factors that alienate one worker from another.

Genesis 3:16 addresses an even greater form of alienation than one's relationship to work. This is the distance experienced even in the most intimate human relationships. Pain is experienced even as we yearn for the beloved. Eve's relationship to Adam is broken. She yearns for him but he remains a source of pain.

Phillip Cary's reflections on God's response to Adam and Eve are instructive:

> To know that they are naked is to know good and evil in
> each other. Much has been said about the self-consciousness
> represented in this moment, which results in their hiding
> themselves rather than walking with God in the garden
> (Gen 3:8). But in addition to self-consciousness there is
> surely also a new consciousness of the other—the one
> whose eyes are open and seeing you. At this moment the
> other becomes an unwelcome presence, troubling and even
> threatening. . . . Each now knows the other as a potential
> source of evil as well as good.[31]

Such new knowledge of the other creates a special type of
agony: desire for the very one who may judge harshly. Adam
and Eve are two aspects of humanity (Gen 1:27). Male and
female yearn for one another at the very core of existence.
Simultaneously, they fear each other. The fear is grounded in
shame, the shame that one may not be seen as delightful in
the eyes of the other.

A shadow falls across all human relationships, including the
most intimate ones. The potential for pain is greatest there because nakedness is essential to the relationship. To be truly seen
is a primary component of erotic love, but it is exactly from that
point that fear emerges. The lover is potential judge who may
find one inadequate, weak, unlovable. And so one hides from the
lover, even as one pursues them.

Our first parents (Adam and Eve) hide from each other even
as they hide from God. In the end, they find no safe harbor in
their love for one another. There abides the potential that such
love may fail, even as we age and face the accompanying physical
changes. Shame fears the loss of love due to the perception of
the other. Americans spend billions of dollars annually to hide

the effects of time, seeking a better face to be perceived by the other. Literally in order to "save face" we go through procedures such as rhinoplasty, chin tucks and Botox injections. Almost none of these procedures are physically necessary. They only exist for the sake of causing a better perception. Shame has created pain as the conclusion to desire.

In contrast, having discovered the answer to shame in Christ, we are able to trust the eyes of the other. Our identity is not granted to us by even those who are closest to us. Our identity and therefore our ultimate value is given to us in Christ. Such a new identity grants the grace necessary for true love. It gives the ability to not fear any other judgment, because they can never be final. This restored identity of *imago Dei* allows us to enjoy otherness as otherness, to delight in the difference. The curse is reversed in Jesus Christ.

What does it mean when we recall that Christ's face was a marred one? Although he dies as a relatively young man, the manner of his death was disfiguring. The Gospels are explicit in referencing the marks of his death, even after his resurrection. What might it mean for us to contemplate Jesus' lack of physical beauty? Or might it be better said that Jesus redefines beauty? "By choosing the broken, weak, despised and foolish face over the idealized face of beauty, Christ (who in Is 53 is prophesied as a wounded, disfigured Messiah) overturns the tables of the Greco-Roman model of physical perfection along with its gods, themselves extensions of this all-too-human notion of bodily perfection."[32] Jesus' redefinition of beauty allows a new confidence for those who fear the passing of beauty that is defined by any other standard. Having one's identity in Christ allows for beautiful faces that may include age lines, large noses and double chins!

Furthermore, how might a redefined beauty allow married couples to behold one another in a more honest and proper manner? Adam and Eve hide from one another as well as from God. But people who have been redefined by gazing into the loving face of Christ provide their mate a freedom that cultural standards deny. "Only eyes trained by gazing continually toward the cross—only eyes cleansed by that second innocence, childlike habitual charity—can see true beauty, true goodness."[33] That gaze alone restores our ability to be "naked and unashamed."

Without Christ's loving gaze, we deeply fear the final judgment of a love that will not last. And yet, relentlessly we still pursue such love. We cling to the notion that the next "true love" will be the one to save us—to grant us respite from our fear of discovery, of exposure. This relentless pursuit of "true love" that casts aside one lover after the next is really a retreat and empowered by shame's victory over us.

THE FINAL JUDGMENT OF LOVE

Perhaps one of the primary indicators of our cultural shift from a guilt to a shame-focused culture is our antipathy toward judgment. We are horrified by the thought that someone out there will view us as less than who we desire to be. We began this book by asking whatever became of the forgiveness of sin. Our conclusion is that our understanding of forgiveness has been clouded by our unwillingness to face the reality of our lives. We cannot tolerate sin language like earlier generations could. Cornelius Plantinga observes, "Some of our grandparents agonized over their sins. A man who lost his temper might wonder whether he could still go to Holy Communion. A woman who for years envied her more attractive and intelligent sister might worry that this sin threatened her very salvation."[34] We so fear rejection that we flee the reality of our lives.

When shame triumphs, is it any surprise that a doctrine of final judgment becomes culturally unpalatable? In contemporary American culture there are few things worse for a person than to be considered judgmental. Therefore, the idea that all of us are on the way toward a final and irreversible judgment is too horrible a thought to be entertained by serious and educated people. That is a conclusion one may draw from a simple cursory view of the media, including much of the Christian media. But what if we have misunderstood the character of the Judge who awaits us?

One of the most moving sections of the *Church Dogmatics* is when Karl Barth takes up the affirmation that Jesus Christ is the "Judge judged in our place."[35] Barth observes that in taking on our sin, God "took it upon Himself as a matter of the care and anxiety and shame and anguish which He accepted in His Son when the Son took to Himself the accusation which was against us."[36] As we complete this study, it is appropriate to add that in the divine work of the triune God, the accuser has become the accused. This then implies the forensic reversal of Romans 8:31-34:

> What then are we to say about these things? If God is for us, who is against us? He who did not withhold his own Son, but gave him up for all of us, will he not with him also give us everything else? Who will bring any charge against God's elect? It is God who justifies. Who is to condemn? It is Christ Jesus, who died, yes, who was raised, who is at the right hand of God, who indeed intercedes for us.

Jesus Christ accomplishes this grand reversal—the shocking courtroom surprise in which the accuser is revealed to be the advocate on behalf of the guilty. It is our shame that frequently inhibits our ability to truly understand the way in which God has dealt with our guilt. Perhaps it is only at this point that Christians ought to contemplate the forensic categories that the apostle employs and that have so dominated the penal substitution model. One dare not think about one's guilt before one comes to understand just how the judicial process has been fixed by a Judge who is judged in our place.

Still, how hard it is to resist the urge to hide from this Judge who sees all. But we need no longer conceal ourselves because this Judge, relentless in pursuit, has already discovered us. The pursuit has taken a circuitous path, ultimately reaching the point wherein the Judge becomes the one who is judged in our place. This Judge has not only pronounced us "not guilty," but has taken the amazing step of healing our shame by restoring our true identity. Looking into the face of Jesus Christ, we behold love. Looking into the face of Jesus Christ, we see our brothers and sisters in a new way. This Judge shall return to judge, but we may now await him "with uplifted head."[37] Barth partially quotes here the Heidelberg Catechism, question 52: "What comfort is it to you that Christ will come to judge the living and the dead? In all my sorrow and persecution I lift up my head and eagerly await as judge from heaven the very same person who before has submitted Himself to the judgment of God for my sake, and has removed all the curse from me." *All* the curse has been removed by the judge who has defeated human shame. And the invitation is extended to all of us now to live lives that are in accord with that gracious judgment.

And so we hear him approaching again. We would hide because we do not feel adequate to meet him. But we remember the face of the one who died, who rose and who even now prays for us. He calls, "Where are you?" And remembering correctly who it is who is calling, we step forth from the shadows, saying, "Amen. Come, Lord Jesus!" (Rev 22:20).

ANSWER TO JANE

And so what do you say to Jane? There she sits, head down, quietly crying. Perhaps you sit in silence for a moment or two and then, making eye contact with her (facing her), humbly offer the following: "Jane, I want you to know something very important. Right here and right now, you are the beloved daughter of God. And the triune God who loves you has done what none of us have the strength to do. In your brother, Jesus, God has forgiven all, even those who do not seek forgiveness. God offers reconciliation to his enemies while they are his enemies. Jane, I want you to know that in my own strength, I simply have no capacity to do that and all that you are admitting to me is that you cannot either. And yet at the same time, here you are confessing to me and obviously showing me how much you wish that you could forgive him.

"What your presence here reveals is that the Holy Spirit is very much active in your life. There is an old term for what you are experiencing: *godly sorrow*. You are experiencing the difference between your own strength and God's promise to you. You could not understand this without the Holy Spirit's work in your life. And that is the same Spirit who unites you to Jesus Christ, the one who did and does forgive his enemies. Through grace alone, Jane, your life is united to his and I have to believe that even now he desires that you rest in his strength. The weakness and inadequacy that you feel in yourself is his call to you to trust only in his forgiving power.

"Furthermore, I want you to know that you are a part of a community of brothers and sisters who also struggle with offering and receiving forgiveness. Allow us to stand with you as you struggle here. None of us are better than you or strong enough to do what it is that you want to do. Allow us to uphold you now even as someday you may have to offer strength to me or someone else in our congregation. You can do that in several ways. You are doing the first one right now: confessing to me, a brother in Christ, a fellow sinner, that you need forgiveness yourself. You already knew that and I already knew that, but by sharing with me here and now, we now know it together in the presence of the Lord who forgives sins. Jane, with joy I remind you that your sins are forgiven!

"Second, I want to encourage you to join one of our new covenant groups that are starting up this month. I think that you will discover there a group of fellow believers who will pray for you and will need you to pray for them. You will discover, I believe, in that group a place where you can be honest because you will find there the love of fellow believers, fellow strugglers. Through your honest struggles, you will discover a new strength because you will catch a glimpse in the faces of your small group members the face of forgiving love: the face of our Lord and Savior, Jesus Christ. It will be in that strength that you will discover a new power that you have never experienced before.

"Finally, Jane, I know that when we struggle, it is easy to skip worship. We just don't feel like we measure up; we feel like hypocrites. But that is exactly the opposite of what we most need to do. When we come together with our fellow believers, our fellow sinners who are saved by grace, we gather to discover and be discovered by the God who loves us. When we offer our praises to the Father, Son and Holy Spirit, we are letting go of our own vain attempts to save ourselves. By coming to worship, we are coming out of hiding in order to meet the God who really does love us.

"Jane, we know this much: Jesus our ascended Lord does not and will not look away from us. He is praying for you and looking at you with eyes of love. Rest in his strength and keep open to the work of forgiveness that he will do in and through you. Never doubt his promise that 'the one who began a good work among you will bring it to completion by the day of Jesus Christ' (Phil 1:6). Would you join me in prayer so that we might return his loving gaze?"

NOTES

ACKNOWLEDGMENTS

[1]Thomas F. Torrance, *Karl Barth: Biblical and Evangelical Theologian* (Edinburgh: T&T Clark, 1990), 239.

[2]C. S. Lewis, *Miracles* (New York: Macmillan Publishing Co., 1978), 94.

CHAPTER 1: WHATEVER HAPPENED TO THE FORGIVENESS OF SINS?

[1]Cornelius Plantinga Jr., *Not the Way It's Supposed to Be: A Breviary of Sin* (Grand Rapids: Eerdmans, 1995), ix.

[2]Ibid., xiii.

[3]Karl Barth, *Church Dogmatics* III/2 (Edinburgh: T&T Clark, 1960), 36.

[4]Ibid.

[5]James B. Torrance, introduction to *The Nature of the Atonement*, by J. McLeod Campbell (Grand Rapids: Eerdmans, 1996), 1.

[6]Ibid.

[7]Andrew Purves, *Reconstructing Pastoral Theology: A Christological Foundation* (Louisville, KY: Westminster John Knox Press, 2004), xxii.

[8]Everett L. Worthington Jr., "Initial Questions About the Art and Science of Forgiving," in *Handbook of Forgiveness*, ed. Everett L. Worthington Jr. (New York: Routledge, 2005), 1.

[9]Michael E. McCullough, Julie Juola Exline and Roy F. Baumeister, "An Annotated Bibliography of Research on Forgiveness and Related Concepts," in *Dimensions of Forgiveness: Psychological Research & Theological Perspectives*, ed. Everett L. Worthington Jr. (Philadelphia: Templeton Foundation Press, 1998), 193-317.

[10]Martin Marty, "The Ethos of Christian Forgiveness," in Worthington, *Dimensions of Forgiveness*, 11.

[11]Torrance, "Introduction," 6.

[12]Eric L. Johnson, ed., *Psychology & Christianity: Five Views* (Downers Grove, IL: IVP Academic, 2010).

[13]The key book for this model is Eric L. Johnson, *Foundations for Soul Care: A Christian Psychology Proposal* (Downers Grove, IL: IVP Academic, 2007).

[14]Barth, *Church Dogmatics* III/2, 132-202.

CHAPTER 2: COVERING OUR NAKEDNESS

[1]Karl Menninger, *Whatever Became of Sin?* (New York: Hawthorne Books, 1973), 228.

[2]Ibid., 38-49.

[3]Philip Rieff, *The Triumph of the Therapeutic* (Chicago: The University of Chicago Press, 1966), 24-25.

[4]Ibid., 261.

[5]Paul Tillich, *The Shaking of the Foundations* (London: SCM Press, 1949), 153-63.

[6]Ibid., 154-55.

[7]Ibid., 161.

[8]Ibid., 162.

[9]Ibid.

[10]E. Brooks Holifield, *A History of Pastoral Care in America: From Salvation to Self-Realization* (Nashville: Abingdon Press, 1983), 332.

[11]George Barna, "Most Adults Feel Accepted by God, but Lack a Biblical Worldview," BarnaGroup, August 9, 2005, www.barna.org/component /content/article/5-barna-update/45-barna-update-sp-657/174-most -adults-feel-accepted-by-god-but-lack-a-biblical-worldview#.Vs3hdPkrLcs.

[12]Tillich, *Shaking*, 163.

[13]Ibid., 159.

[14]James Hillman and Michael Ventura, *We've Had a Hundred Years of Psychotherapy and the World's Getting Worse* (New York: Harper, 1993), 3-4.

[15]Christian Smith and Melina Lundquist Denton, *Soul Searching: The Religious and Spiritual Lives of American Teenagers* (New York: Oxford University Press, 2009).

[16]Robert Enright, *Forgiveness Is a Choice* (Washington, DC: American Psychological Association, 2001).

[17]Ibid., 133.

[18]Everett L. Worthington Jr., *A Just Forgiveness* (Downers Grove, IL: Inter-Varsity Press, 2009), 74-75.

[19]Ibid., 77.

[20]Ibid., 78.

[21]Ibid., 107.

[22]I will argue in chapter five that the triune God experiences the brokenness of relationship in order to reconcile to world to himself. This is most fully revealed on the cross. The act of forgiveness is not an end in itself but is the necessary prelude to reconciliation.

[23]Everett L. Worthington Jr., *Forgiving and Reconciling: Bridges to Wholeness and Hope* (Downers Grove, IL: InterVarsity Press, 2003), 174. The language of *mirroring* is itself problematic. Kathryn Tanner has effectively demonstrated how the doctrine of the Trinity actually does little to illumine how we relate to God or to one another. The perfect relating of Father, Son and Holy Spirit taken as a type of model can only be a judgment on our broken relationships. Instead, it is the doctrine of the incarnation, the union of human and divine natures in Jesus Christ, that reveals how we may relate to one another in union with him. See Kathryn Tanner, *Christ the Key* (Cambridge: Cambridge University Press, 2010), particularly chapter five, "Politics."

[24]Worthington, *Forgiving and Reconciling*, 174.

[25]What may lead to some of Worthington's confusion is his understanding of the relationship between theology and psychology. He has explicated his thought in *Coming to Peace with Psychology* (Downers Grove, IL: IVP Academic, 2010). Like many social scientists, however, Worthington often fails to understand the philosophical presuppositions of his own discipline. For a critique of this common problem, see Don S. Browning and Terry D. Cooper, *Religious Thought and Modern Psychologies*, 2nd ed. (Minneapolis: Fortress Press, 2004) and Christian Smith, *The Sacred Project of American Sociology* (New York: Oxford University Press, 2014). Furthermore, one may argue that Worthington too easily discounts the noetic effect of sin. He is quite convinced that psychology better establishes the truth of human nature. See *Coming to Peace*, 137-45.

[26]Eric L. Johnson, *Foundations for Soul Care* (Downers Grove, IL: IVP Academic, 2007), 97.

[27]Ray S. Anderson, *The Soul of Ministry* (Louisville, KY: Westminster John Knox Press, 1997), 6.

[28]Fraser Watts and Liz Gulliford, *Forgiveness in Context* (New York: T&T Clark, 2004), 65.

[29]As I write this, the United States has just experienced the horror of the murder of nine African Americans at the Emanuel AME Church in Charleston, South Carolina. One of the victims was seventy-year-old Ethel Lance. At the accused murderer's hearing, her daughter, Nadine Collier, said to him, "You took something very precious away from me. I will never talk to her again. I will never be able to hold her again. But I forgive you. And have mercy on your soul." www.nytimes.com/2015/06/20 /us/charleston-shooting-dylann-storm-roof.html?_r=o. It is doubtful indeed that the immediate benefits of forgiveness matter much in a context such as this one.

[30]Thomas F. Torrance, *Conflict and Agreement in the Church*, vol. 2 (Eugene, OR: Wipf & Stock, 1996), 159.

[31]Ibid.

[32]Ibid.

[33]Ibid., 160.

[34]We will delve more deeply into this below when we take up the problem of the Latin heresy. The Latin heresy, by turning the atonement into an external transaction between humanity and God, places too great an emphasis on the human response to what God has done in Christ.

[35]It is apparent that the first disciples only truly realize who Christ is and what he has accomplished after his ascension to the Father and the Holy Spirit is given at Pentecost.

[36]Dietrich Bonhoeffer, *Creation and Fall: A Theological Exposition of Genesis 1–3* (Minneapolis: Fortress Press, 1996), 139, 140.

[37]Josef Breuer and Sigmund Freud, *Studies on Hysteria* (New York: Basic Books, 1955), 305.

CHAPTER 3: GUILT AND SHAME

[1]Karl Barth, *Church Dogmatics* III/2 (Edinburgh: T&T Clark, 1960).

[2]Ibid., 71-131.

[3]Ibid., 198.

[4]See below for a discussion of penal substitution.

[5]These folks are occasionally referred to as the *dones* in distinction with

the *nones.* If the nones practice no organized religion, the dones are the former (often strongly committed) practitioners. The dones seem often to feel acutely the absence of their religion.

[6]Martin Buber, "Guilt and Guilt Feelings," in *Martin Buber on Psychology and Psychotherapy*, ed. Judith Buber Agassi (Syracuse: Syracuse University Press, 1999), 110-38.

[7]Mt 6:12; Lk 11:4.

[8]Carl D. Schneider, "Shame," in *Dictionary of Pastoral Care and Counseling*, ed. Rodney J. Hunter (Nashville: Abingdon Press, 2005), 1160.

[9]Leland Ryken, James C. Wilhoit and Tremper Longman III, eds., *Dictionary of Biblical Imagery* (Downers Grove, IL: InterVarsity Press, 1998), 355-56.

[10]E. V. Stein, "Guilt," in Hunter, *Dictionary of Pastoral Care and Counseling*, 489.

[11]These are the famous oedipal issues, etc. For a general introduction, see Ana-Maria Rizzuto, *The Birth of the Living God: A Psychoanalytic Study* (Chicago: The University of Chicago Press, 1981).

[12]Bruce S. Narramore, *No Condemnation: Rethinking Guilt Motivation in Counseling, Preaching & Parenting* (Grand Rapids: Zondervan, 1984).

[13]The three theorists are Freud, Fromm and Mowrer; see ibid., 83-130.

[14]Ibid., 142.

[15]Ibid., 145-46.

[16]For an interesting discussion, see Thom Schultz, "The Rise of the 'Done with Church' Population," *ChurchLeaders*, www.churchleaders.com/outreach -missions/outreach-missions-articles/177144-thom-schultz-rise-of-the -done-with-church-population.html.

[17]Narramore, *No Condemnation*, 33.

[18]Schneider, "Shame," 1161.

[19]For a good discussion of this topic, see John C. Hoffman's *Ethical Confrontation in Counseling* (Chicago: University of Chicago Press, 1979).

[20]Schneider, "Shame," 1161.

[21]June Price Tangney and Ronda L. Dearing, *Shame and Guilt* (New York: The Guilford Press, 2002).

[22]Ibid., 3.

[23]Schneider, "Shame," 1160.

[24]Tangney and Dearing, *Shame and Guilt*, 24.

[25]Gershen Kaufman, *Shame: The Power of Caring* (Rochester, VT: Schenkman Books, 1992), 79-97.

[26]Michael Mangis, *Signature Sins: Taming Our Wayward Hearts* (Downers Grove, IL: InterVarsity Press, 2008).

[27]Adam J. Johnson, *Atonement: A Guide for the Perplexed* (New York: Bloomsbury/T&T Clark, 2015), 32.

[28]Ibid., 34.

[29]Adam Johnson points out how important it is to differentiate between the reality of what Christ accomplishes on our behalf and the theories that Christian theologians have used to describe it. All too often, the theories have functioned as a procrustean bed, forcing the reality to fit the theory. Ibid., 37.

[30]Gustaf Aulen, *Christus Victor* (New York: Macmillan, 1969).

[31]Johnson, *Atonement*, 167-68, points out that there really is no unified theory of atonement, but rather a group of theories. At the same time, as ancient as the theories of ransom are, they are still helpful in that they focus on both individual and collective aspects of sin.

[32]Kathryn Tanner, *Christ the Key* (Cambridge: Cambridge University Press, 2010).

[33]Ibid., 248.

[34]The dominance of the theory in the Western church eventually "calcified into a more stringent affirmation of penal substitution as the 'one and only correct way of talking about the atonement.'" Johnson, *Atonement*, 110.

[35]Thomas F. Torrance, *Karl Barth: Biblical and Evangelical Theologian* (Edinburgh: T&T Clark, 1990), 213-40.

[36]Since at least Leo the Great (400–461) the Western church has taught "that the Son of God, assumed neutral human nature, that is, human nature unaffected by sin and guilt, and therefore not under the divine judgement. This meant that in the atonement Christ could be thought of only as assuming our actual sin, but not our original sin, and then only by way of some external or moral forensic transaction." Ibid., 203.

Chapter 4: Opened Eyes and Downturned Faces

[1]Dietrich Bonhoeffer, *Creation and Fall*, Dietrich Bonhoeffer Works, vol. 3 (Minneapolis: Fortress Press, 1997), 107. In what follows, I will utilize a number of Bonhoeffer's insights to help us better understand Gen 3 and 4 in the light of the shame/guilt distinction.

[2]"'You will not die at all.' 'You shall die.' These two statements mark the cleavage that now splits the world apart for Adam. . . . Truth against

truth—God's truth against the serpent's truth. God's truth tied to the prohibition, the serpent's truth tied to the promise, God's truth pointing to my limit, the serpent's truth pointing to my unlimitedness—both of them truth, that is, both originating with God, God against God. . . . *Imago dei*—humankind in the image of God in being for God and the neighbor, in its original creatureliness and limitedness; *sicut deus*—humankind similar to God in knowing-out-of-its-own-self about good and evil. . . . *Imago dei*—bound to the word of the Creator and deriving life from the Creator; *sicut deus*—bound to the depths of its own knowledge of God, of good and evil. *Imago dei*—the creature living in the unity of obedience; *sicut deus*—the creator-human-being who lives on the basis of the divide between good and evil. *Imago dei, sicut deus, agnus dei*—the human being who is God incarnate, who was sacrificed for humankind *sicut deus*, in true divinity slaying its false divinity and restoring the *imago dei.*" Ibid., 113. Here Bonhoeffer masterfully outlines the only meaningful differences for all of humanity. In eating the fruit of the tree, Adam and Eve trade relationship for knowledge. *Imago Dei* (humans bearing God's image) appears tied to prohibitions, limits and neighbors. By necessity one must live beyond the self and what the self can do for itself. *Sicut deus* is tied to false promises of limitlessness and ultimately abides alone. For that self cannot leave judgment to any other but must always fall back on its own understanding.

[3]Ibid., 124.

[4]Barth, *Church Dogmatics* III/2 (Edinburgh: T&T Clark, 1960), 36.

[5]These attempts might put us in mind of the work of Gershen Kaufman, *Shame: The Power of Caring* (Rochester, VT: Schenkman Books, 1992), which we explored in the last chapter.

[6]"Humankind, which has fallen away from God in a precipitous plunge, now still flees from God. For humankind the fall is not enough; its flight cannot be fast enough. This flight, Adam's hiding away from God, we call conscience. Before the fall there was no conscience. Only since humankind has become divided from the Creator are human beings divided within themselves. . . . Here, far away from God, humankind itself plays the role of being judge and in this way seeks to evade God's judgment. Humankind now lives truly out of the resources of its own good and evil, its own innermost dividedness from itself. Conscience means feeling shame before God; at the same time one conceals one's own wickedness

in shame, humankind in shame justifies itself—and yet, on the other hand, at the same time there is in shame an unintentional recognition of the other person. Conscience is not the voice of God within sinful human beings; instead it is precisely their defense against this voice." Bonhoeffer, *Creation and Fall*, 128.

[7]John Watson, *Shame* (London: Grove Books, 2005), 6.

[8]"So instead of standing before God, Adam falls back on the trick learned from the serpent of correcting what is in God's mind, of appealing from God the Creator to a better God, a different God. . . . He has appealed to his conscience, to his knowledge of good and evil, and on the basis of this knowledge accused his Creator. He has not recognized the grace of the Creator that shows itself precisely in that God calls Adam and does not let him flee. Instead Adam sees this grace only as hate, as wrath, a wrath that inflames his own hate, his rebellion, his desire to get away from God. Adam keeps on falling. The fall drops with increasing speed for an immeasurable distance." Bonhoeffer, *Creation and Fall*, 129-30.

[9]"God speaks to Adam and halts him in his flight. Come out of your hiding place, out of your self-reproach, out of your cover-up, out of your secrecy, out of your self-torment, out of your vain remorse. Confess who you are, do not lose yourself in religious despair, be yourself." Ibid., 128.

[10]"Cain is the first human being who is born on the ground that is cursed. It is with Cain that history begins, the history of death. . . . The end of Cain's history, and so the end of all history . . . is Christ on the cross, the murdered Son of God. That is the last desperate assault on the gate of paradise. . . . What a strange paradise is this hill of Golgotha, this cross, this blood, this broken body. What a strange tree of life, this trunk on which the very God had to suffer and die." Ibid., 145-46.

[11]See above in chapter three.

[12]Gerhard von Rad, *Genesis* (Philadelphia: The Westminster Press, 1972), 105.

[13]Walter Brueggemann, *Genesis* (Atlanta: John Knox Press, 1982), 63.

[14]Dietrich Bonhoeffer, *Ethics* (New York: Collier Books, 1965), 20.

CHAPTER 5: THE SHAME OF THE CROSS

[1]Ruth Leys, *From Guilt to Shame* (Princeton: Princeton University Press, 2007).

[2]Ibid., 183.

[3]Giorgio Agamben, *Remnants of Auschwitz* (New York: Zone Books, 2002).

[4]Leys, *From Guilt to Shame*, 7.

[5]William Shakespeare, *Julius Caesar* I, ii. 141-42.

[6]Arguably, Levi did not survive the Holocaust. He was a later victim when he took his own life in 1987.

[7]Primo Levi, *The Drowned and the Saved* (New York: Vintage Books, 1988).

[8]Ibid., 72-73.

[9]Ibid., 74.

[10]Ibid., 78.

[11]"Are you ashamed because you are alive in the place of another? And in particular, of a man more generous, more sensitive, more useful, wiser, worthier of living than you? You cannot block out such feelings: you examine yourself, you review your memories, hoping to find them all, and that none of them are masked or disguised. No, you find no obvious transgressions, you did not usurp anyone's place, you did not beat anyone (but would you have had the strength to do so?), you did not steal anyone's bread, nevertheless you cannot exclude it." Ibid., 81.

[12]Ibid.

[13]Ibid., 78.

[14]Mark D. Baker, ed., *Proclaiming the Scandal of the Cross* (Grand Rapids: Baker Academic, 2006) and C. Norman Kraus, *Jesus Christ Our Lord* (Eugene, OR: Wipf & Stock, 1990).

[15]Seventy years after the end of World War II, we in the West are still amazed at the nation of Japan's hesitancy and unwillingness to accept the guilt of war crimes. However, we should not be surprised that a shame-centered culture such as Japan's lacks the capacity to accept guilt. Only the strong and victorious are able to really accept guilt for their moral failures.

[16]Jürgen Moltmann, *The Crucified God* (New York: Harper and Row, 1974), 246.

[17]In what follows I will be utilizing the four canonical Gospels for what is commonly known as the "seven last words from the cross." No doubt, each of the Gospel authors has his own reasons for including what he does. I am not interested here in why Luke quotes this or John quotes that. Instead, it is my aim to see how all seven sayings together grant us a fuller picture of what is occurring in Jesus' final agonizing hours. Together, the four accounts allow us to better understand what God is doing.

[18]Augustine, *The Trinity*, trans. Stephen McKenna (Washington, DC: Catholic University Press, 1963), 503.

[19]Even though verse 24 ends Psalm 22 with hope ("For he did not despise or abhor the affliction of the afficted; he did not hide his face from me, but heard when I cried to him," Ps 22:24) there is no reason to speculate that Jesus is being hopeful. To understand the depths of God's love on display in the cross, it seems to make better sense to allow the cry of anguish to be just that, a cry of hopelessness and despair!

[20]Note well: even in this human, all too human, cry Jesus is dying as a faithful Jewish man. He is still searching for the God of Israel in the only other way that he would know: the holy writings.

[21]Joachim Jeremias, *The Prayers of Jesus* (Philadelphia: Fortress Press, 1978), 55.

[22]I am well aware of the ancient church's reluctance to speak of the suffering of God the Father. Patripassianism was rejected because of the way in which it blurred the distinctiveness of the three divine persons. However, to maintain that the Father suffers exactly as the Son is not the same thing as to avow that the Father suffers. Moltmann does a good job in delineating the unique difference between the Father's suffering and the Son's. Moltmann, *Crucified God*, 240-49.

[23]It should not surprise us that the distancing of shame is surmounted by the love that exists eternally within the Godhead. Hans Urs von Balthasar notes that the very begetting of the Son by the Father allows for any other distance to occur within God. "This divine act that brings forth the Son, that is, the second way of participating in (and of being) the identical Godhead, involves the positing of an absolute, infinite 'distance' that can contain and embrace all the other distances that are possible within the world of finitude, including the distance of sin." *Theo-Drama: Theological Dramatic Theory*, vol. 4, *The Action* (San Francisco: Ignatius Press, 1994), 323. Again, this helps us understand the incarnational nature of the atonement. The Son of God's taking on of human flesh was a distancing that was simultaneously a display of the eternal love that cannot be overcome. Even the shaming distance experienced by all three divine persons on the cross must be understood as a display of the eternal love now brought to broken humanity to eliminate the sinful distance created by our rebellion, a rebellion manifested in our desire to be "like God" without the love.

CHAPTER 6: "AS ONE FROM WHOM OTHERS HIDE THEIR FACES . . ."

[1]Martin Hengel, *Crucifixion* (Philadelphia: Fortress Press, 1977).

[2]Unlike other examples of the Adonis myth (a young man dying in a redemptive manner for his people) there is no particular emphasis on what sort of death the young man must die.

[3]Hengel, *Crucifixion*, 10.

[4]Martyrdom—the Greek word for "witness"—inspires by means of observation. A martyrdom has no power without its observation. Only those who behold such a death are convinced by the truth of the witness. A contemporary example is the 2015 martyrdom of the twenty Egyptians at the hands of ISIS. There was a twenty-first captive, an African nonbeliever, who when offered the opportunity to avoid death, embraced it instead, saying that "their (the Coptic Christians) God is my God." "2015 Kidnapping and Beheading of Copys in Libya," *Wikipedia*, https://en .wikipedia.org/wiki/2015_kidnapping_and_beheading_of_Copts_in_ Libya (captured on August 26, 2015). And yet, here is a death from which the human tendency is to look away.

[5]Hengel, *Crucifixion*, 18.

[6]Interestingly, both ancient Docetism and Islam have deep respect for Jesus and simultaneously find the death of Christ on a cross to be abhorrent.

[7]Hengel, *Crucifixion*, 86-90.

[8]Ibid., 87. Emphasis added.

[9]Paul is "expressing the harsh experience of his missionary preaching and the offense that it caused, in particular the experience of his preaching among non-Jews. . . . The reason why in his letters he talks about the cross above all in a polemical context is that he deliberately wants to provoke his opponents, who are attempting to water down the offense caused by the cross. Jesus did not die a gentle death like Socrates, with his cup of hemlock, much less passing on 'old and full of years' like the patriarchs of the Old Testament. Rather, he died like a slave or a common criminal, in torment, on the tree of shame. . . . The particular form of the death of Jesus, the man and the messiah, represents a scandal which people would like to blunt, remove or domesticate in any way possible." Ibid., 89-90.

[10]Raymond Brown, *The Death of the Messiah* (New York: Doubleday, 1993), 577.

[11]David Ford, *Self and Salvation: Being Transformed* (New York: Cambridge University Press, 1999), 17.

[12]F. LeRon Shults and Steven J. Sandage, *The Faces of Forgiveness* (Grand Rapids: Baker Academic, 2003), 18.

[13]Ford, *Self and Salvation*, 18.

[14]Ibid.

[15]See chapter three.

[16]See below, in chapter seven, how the wounded face of Christ has the power to transform and redefine beauty.

[17]"Beautiful humanity is the reflection of the essence of God in His kindness towards men as it appeared in Jesus Christ (Tit. 34). In this self-declaration, however, God's beauty embraces death as well as life, fear as well as joy, what we might call the ugly as well as what we might call the beautiful. It reveals itself and wills to be known on the road from the one to the other, in the turning from the self-humiliation of God for the benefit of man to the exaltation of man by God and to God. This turning is the mystery of the name of Jesus Christ and of the glory revealed in this name." Karl Barth, *Church Dogmatics* II/2 (Edinburgh: T&T Clark, 1957), 665.

[18]"Who knows it except the man to whom it gives the power to know it? And how can it be known except in the face of Him who Himself gives us power to know it? There is no other face of this kind. No other face is the self-declaration of the divine loving-kindness towards men. No other speaks at the same time of the human suffering of the true God and the divine glory of the true man. This is the function of the face of Jesus Christ alone." Ibid., 665-66.

[19]"If the beauty of Christ is sought in a glorious Christ who is not the crucified, the search will always be in vain. But who does not do this? And who finds it at this point? Who of himself does not find the opposite here? Who sees and believes that the One who has been abased is the One who is exalted, that this very man is very God? The glory and beauty of God shines out in this unity and differentiation. In this it persuades, convinces and conquers. This unity and differentiation is God's καλόν (beauty) which itself has the power of a καλεῖν (call). It is the beauty which Solomon did not have, but which with all his equipment he could only prophesy. It is the beauty of which we must also say that even Athens with all its beautiful humanity did not have and could not even prophesy it, because unlike Jerusalem it thought it had it." Ibid., 665.

[20]Adam J. Johnson, *Atonement: A Guide for the Perplexed* (New York: Bloomsbury/T&T Clark, 2015), 138.

[21]Robert Enright, *Forgiveness Is a Choice* (Washington, DC: American Psychological Association, 2001), 157.

[22]Miroslav Volf, *Exclusion and Embrace* (Nashville: Abingdon Press, 1996), 125.

CHAPTER 7: LIVING BEFORE CHRIST'S FACE

[1]Kenneth E. Bailey, *Poet and Peasant* (Grand Rapids: Eerdmans, 1976), 158-206.

[2]David F. Ford, *Self and Salvation: Being Transformed* (New York: Cambridge University Press, 1999), 176.

[3]Helmut Thielicke, *Our Heavenly Father* (New York: Harper and Row, 1960), 107.

[4]L. Gregory Jones, *Embodying Forgiveness* (Grand Rapids: Eerdmans, 1995), xii.

[5]Robert Karen, "Shame," *The Atlantic*, February 1992, 70.

[6]Dietrich Bonhoeffer, *Spiritual Care* (Philadelphia: Fortress Press, 1985), 62.

[7]Ibid.

[8]Max Thurian, *Confession* (London: SCM Press, 1958).

[9]Ibid., 23, 24.

[10]Ibid., 28.

[11]Ibid., 55-56.

[12]Ibid., 105.

[13]Ibid., 115.

[14]Ibid., 120.

[15]Ibid., 124.

[16]Eduard Thurneysen, *A Theology of Pastoral Care* (Richmond: John Knox Press, 1962), 309-14.

[17]Ibid., 311.

[18]Louis L. Martz, ed., *George Herbert and Henry Vaughn* (New York: Oxford University Press, 1986), 99.

[19]Charles Williams, *The Forgiveness of Sins* (Grand Rapids: Eerdmans, 1942), 14.

[20]Edward P. Wimberly, *No Shame in Wesley's Gospel* (Eugene, OR: Wipf & Stock, 2011), 68.

[21]John Wesley, "A Plain Account of the People Called Methodists," *The*

Works of John Wesley, vol. 9, ed. Rupert E. Davies (Nashville: Abingdon Press, 1989), 266.

[22]Ibid.

[23]Ibid., 266-67.

[24]Ibid., 78.

[25]See the discussion of Bruce S. Narramore's work in chapter three.

[26]Charles Wesley, "O for a Thousand Tongues to Sing," *United Methodist Hymnal* (Nashville: Abingdon Press, 1989), #57.

[27]Stephanie Rosenbloom, "Honk If You Adore My Child, Too," *The New York Times*, January 5, 2006, www.nytimes.com/2006/01/05/fashion/thursdaystyles/05boasting.html?pagewanted=all&_r=0.

[28]Austin Farrer, *The End of Man* (Grand Rapids: Eerdmans, 1974), 28-29.

[29]Karl Barth, *The Epistle to the Romans*, trans. Edwyn C. Hoskyns, 6th ed. (New York: Oxford University Press, 1968), 317.

[30]Barry Schwartz, "Rethinking Work," *New York Times*, August 30, 2015, www.nytimes.com/2015/08/30/opinion/sunday/rethinking-work.html?_r=0.

[31]Philip Cary, "Knowing the Other," *First Things*, January 2, 2014, www.firstthings.com/blogs/firstthoughts/2014/01/knowing-the-other.

[32]Bruce Herman, "Wounds and Beauty," in *The Beauty of God: Theology and the Arts*, ed. Daniel J. Treier, Mark Husbands and Roger Lundin (Downers Grove, IL: IVP Academic, 2007), 118.

[33]Ibid., 119.

[34]Cornelius Plantinga Jr., *Not the Way It's Supposed to Be: A Breviary of Sin* (Grand Rapids: Eerdmans, 1995), ix.

[35]Karl Barth, *Church Dogmatics* IV/1, *The Doctrine of Reconciliation* (Edinburgh: T&T Clark, 1956), 211-83.

[36]Ibid., 242.

[37]Ibid., 211.

BIBLIOGRAPHY

Agamben, Giorgio. *Remnants of Auschwitz*. New York: Zone Books, 2002.

Anderson, Gary. *Sin: A History*. New Haven: Yale University Press, 2009.

Anderson, Ray S. *The Soul of Ministry*. Louisville: Westminster John Knox Press, 1997.

Augustine. *The Trinity*. Translated by Stephen McKenna. Washington, DC: Catholic University Press, 1963.

Aulen, Gustaf. *Christus Victor*. New York: Macmillan, 1969.

Bailey, Kenneth E. *Poet and Peasant*. Grand Rapids: Eerdmans, 1976.

Baker, Mark D., ed. *Proclaiming the Scandal of the Cross*. Grand Rapids: Baker Academic, 2006.

Balthasar, Hans Urs von. *Theo-Drama: Theological Dramatic Theory*. Vol. 4, *The Action*. San Francisco: Ignatius Press, 1994.

Barna, George. "Most Adults Feel Accepted by God, but Lack a Biblical Worldview." BarnaGroup. August 9, 2005. www.barna.org /barna-update/article/5-barna-update/174-most-adults-feel-ac cepted-by-god-but-lack-a-biblical-worldview#.U9_afmPG9gs.

Barth, Karl. *The Christian Life*. Translated by Geoffrey W. Bromiley. Grand Rapids: Eerdmans, 1981.

———. *Church Dogmatics* II/1. Translated by T. H. L. Parker, W. B. Johnston, Harold Knight and J. L. M Haire. Edinburgh: T&T Clark, 1957.

———. *Church Dogmatics* III/2. Translated by Harold Knight, G. W. Bromiley, J. K. S. Reid and R. H. Fuller. Edinburgh: T&T Clark, 1960.

———. *Church Dogmatics* IV/1. Translated by G. W. Bromiley. Edinburgh: T&T Clark, 1956.

———. *Church Dogmatics* IV/2. Translated by G. W. Bromiley. Edinburgh: T&T Clark, 1958.

———. *Church Dogmatics* IV/3. Translated by G. W. Bromiley. Edinburgh: T&T Clark, 1961.

———. *The Epistle to the Romans.* Translated by Edwyn C. Hoskyns. 6th ed. New York: Oxford University Press, 1968.

Bonhoeffer, Dietrich. *Creation and Fall.* Dietrich Bonhoeffer Works, vol. 3. Minneapolis: Fortress Press, 1997.

———. *Ethics.* New York: Collier Books, 1965.

———. *Spiritual Care.* Philadelphia: Fortress Press, 1985.

Breuer, Josef, and Sigmund Freud. *Studies on Hysteria.* New York: Basic Books, 1955.

Brown, Raymond. *The Death of the Messiah.* New York: Doubleday, 1993.

Browning, Don S., and Terry D. Cooper. *Religious Thought & Modern Psychologies.* 2nd ed. Minneapolis: Fortress Press, 2004.

Brueggemann, Walter. *Genesis.* Atlanta: John Knox Press, 1982.

Buber, Martin. "Guilt and Guilt Feelings." In *Martin Buber on Psychology and Psychotherapy*, ed. Judith Buber Agassi. Syracuse: Syracuse University Press, 1999.

Campbell, J. McLeod. *The Nature of the Atonement.* Grand Rapids: Eerdmans, 1996.

Capps, Donald. *The Depleted Self.* Minneapolis: Fortress Press, 1993.

Cary, Philip. "Knowing the Other." *First Things*, January 2, 2014. www .firstthings.com/blogs/firstthoughts/2014/01/02/knowing-the-other/.

Colyer, Elmer. *How to Read T. F. Torrance.* Downers Grove, IL: InterVarsity Press, 2001.

Cooper, Terry D. *Sin, Pride & Self-Acceptance.* Downers Grove, IL: InterVarsity Press, 2003.

Enright, Robert. *Forgiveness Is a Choice*. Washington, DC: American Psychological Association, 2001.

Farrer, Austin. *The End of Man*. Grand Rapids: Eerdmans, 1974.

Ford, David F. *Self and Salvation: Being Transformed*. New York: Cambridge University Press, 1999.

Ford, David F., and Daniel W Hardy. *Jubilate: Theology in Praise*. London: Dartman, Longman and Todd, 1984.

Hengel, Martin. *Crucifixion*. Philadelphia: Fortress Press, 1977.

Hillman, James, and Michael Ventura. *We've Had a Hundred Years of Psychotherapy and the World's Getting Worse*. New York: Harper, 1993.

Hoffman, John C. *Ethical Confrontation in Counseling*. Chicago: The University of Chicago Press, 1979.

Holifield, E. Brooks. *A History of Pastoral Care in America: From Salvation to Self-Realization*. Nashville: Abingdon Press, 1983.

Jeremias, Joachim. *The Prayers of Jesus*. Philadelphia: Fortress Press, 1978.

Johnson, Eric L. *Foundations for Soul Care: A Christian Psychology Proposal*. Downers Grove, IL: InterVarsity Press, 2007.

———, ed. *Psychology and Christianity: Five Views*. Downers Grove, IL: InterVarsity Press, 2010.

Jones, L. Gregory. *Embodying Forgiveness: A Theological Analysis*. Grand Rapids: Eerdmans, 1995.

Karen, Robert. "Shame." *The Atlantic*, February 1992.

Kaufman, Gershen. *Shame: The Power of Caring*. Rochester, VT: Schenkman Books, Inc., 1992.

Kraus, C. Norman. *Jesus Christ Our Lord*. Eugene, OR: Wipf & Stock, 1990.

Levi, Primo. *The Drowned and the Saved*. New York: Vintage Books, 1988.

Lewis, C. S. *Miracles*. New York: MacMillan Publishing Co., 1978.

Leys, Ruth. *From Guilt to Shame*. Princeton: Princeton University Press, 2007.

Mangis, Michael. *Signature Sins: Taming Our Wayward Hearts*. Downers Grove, IL: InterVarsity Press, 2008.

Martz, Louis L., ed. *George Herbert and Henry Vaughn*. New York: Oxford University Press, 1986.

McCullough, Michael E., Julie Juola Exline and Roy F. Baumeister. "An Annotated Bibliography of Research on Forgiveness and Related Concepts." In *Dimensions of Forgiveness: Psychological Research & Theological Perspectives*, ed. Everett L. Worthington Jr., 193-317. Philadelphia: Templeton Foundation Press, 1998.

Menninger, Karl. *Whatever Became of Sin?* New York: Hawthorne Books, 1973.

Moltmann, Jürgen. *The Crucified God*. New York: Harper and Row, 1974.

Narramore, S. Bruce. *No Condemnation: Rethinking Guilt Motivation in Counseling, Preaching & Parenting*. Grand Rapids: Zondervan, 1984.

Pattison, Stephen. *Shame: Theory, Therapy, Theology*. New York: Cambridge University Press, 2000.

Plantinga, Cornelius, Jr. *Not the Way It's Supposed to Be: A Breviary of Sin*. Grand Rapids: Eerdmans, 1995.

Purves, Andrew. *Reconstructing Pastoral Theology: A Christological Foundation*. Louisville: Westminster John Knox, 2004.

Rieff, Philip. *The Triumph of the Therapeutic: Uses of Faith After Freud*. Chicago: The University of Chicago Press, 1966.

Rizutto, Ana-Maria. *The Birth of the Living God: A Psychoanalytic Study*. Chicago: The University of Chicago Press, 1981.

Ryken, Leland, James C. Wilhoit and Tremper Longman III. *Dictionary of Biblical Imagery*. Downers Grove, IL: InterVarsity Press, 1998.

Schneider, Carl D. "Shame." In *Dictionary of Pastoral Care and Counseling*, ed. Rodney J. Hunter. Nashville: Abingdon Press, 2005.

———. *Shame, Exposure, and Privacy*. New York: W. W. Norton & Co., 1977.

Schultz, Thom. "The Rise of the 'Done with Church' Population." *ChurchLeaders*. www.churchleaders.com/outreach-missions/out reach-missions-articles/177144-thom-schultz-rise-of-the-done-with -church-population.html.

Schwartz, Barry. "Rethinking Work." *New York Times*, August 30, 2015. www.nytimes.com/2015/08/30/opinion/sunday/rethinking-work .html?_r=0.

Shults, F. LeRon, and Steven J. Sandage. *The Faces of Forgiveness*. Grand Rapids: Baker Academic, 2003.

Smith, Christian. *The Sacred Project of American Sociology*. New York: Oxford University Press, 2014.

Smith, Christian, and Melina Lundquist Denton. *Soul Searching: The Religious and Spiritual Lives of American Teenagers*. New York: Oxford University Press, 2009.

Stein, E. V. "Guilt." In *Dictionary of Pastoral Care and Counseling*, ed. Rodney J. Hunter. Nashville: Abingdon Press, 2005.

Tangney, June Price, and Ronda L. Dearing. *Shame and Guilt*. New York: The Guilford Press, 2002.

Tanner, Kathryn. *Christ the Key*. Cambridge: Cambridge University Press, 2010.

Thielicke, Helmut. *Our Heavenly Father*. New York: Harper and Row, Publishers, 1960.

Thurian, Max. *Confession*. London: SCM Press, 1958.

Thurneysen, Eduard. *A Theology of Pastoral Care*. Richmond: John Knox Press, 1962.

Tillich, Paul. *The Shaking of the Foundations*. London: SCM Press, 1949.

Torrance, Thomas F. *Conflict and Agreement in the Church*. Vol. 2. Eugene, OR: Wipf & Stock, 1996.

———. *Karl Barth: Biblical and Evangelical Theologian*. Edinburgh: T&T Clark, 1990.

Treier, Daniel J., Mark Husbands and Roger Lundin. *The Beauty of God: Theology and the Arts*. Downers Grove, IL: IVP Academic, 2007.

Volf, Miroslav. *Exclusion and Embrace*. Nashville: Abingdon Press, 1996.

von Rad, Gerhard. *Genesis*. Philadelphia: The Westminster Press, 1972.

Watson, John. *Shame*. London: Grove Books, 2005.

Watts, Fraser. "Shame, Sin and Guilt." In *Forgiveness and Truth: Explorations in Contemporary Theology*, ed. Alistair McFadyen and Marcel Sarot. Edinburgh: T&T Clark, 2001.

Watts, Fraser, and Liz Gulliford. *Forgiveness in Context: Theology and Psychology in Creative Dialogue*. New York: T&T Clark, 2004.

Wesley, John. "A Plain Account of the People Called Methodists." In *The Works of John Wesley*. Vol. 9, edited by Rupert E. Davies. Nashville: Abingdon Press, 1989.

Williams, Charles. *The Forgiveness of Sins*. Grand Rapids: Eerdmans, 1942.

Wimberly, Edward P. *No Shame in Wesley's Gospel*. Eugene, OR: Wipf & Stock, 2011.

Worthington, Everett L., Jr. *Coming to Peace with Psychology*. Downers Grove, IL: IVP Academic, 2010.

———, ed. *Dimensions of Forgiveness*. Philadelphia: Templeton Foundation Press, 1998.

———. *Forgiving and Reconciling: Bridges to Wholeness and Hope*. Downers Grove, IL: InterVarsity Press, 2003.

———. "Initial Questions About the Art and Science of Forgiving." In *Handbook of Forgiveness*, ed. Everett L. Worthington Jr., 1-14. New York: Routledge, 2005.

———. *A Just Forgiveness*. Downers Grove, IL: InterVarsity Press, 2009.

GENERAL INDEX

SCRIPTURE INDEX

Finding the Textbook You Need